The Lighter Side Part 2

A Former NHS Paramedic's Selection of Humorous Mess Room Tales

Andy Thompson

Digital, Paperback and Hardcover editions first published in March 2021 by emp3books, Norwood House, Elvetham Road, Fleet, GU51 4HL, England.

ISBN: 978-1-910734-42-1

Also Available in Digital, Paperback, Hardcover and Audible

The Dark Side
Real Life Accounts of an NHS Paramedic
The Good, the Bad and the Downright Ugly

The Dark Side
Part 2
Real Life Accounts of an NHS Paramedic
The Traumatic, the Tragic and the Tearful

The Lighter Side
An NHS Paramedic's Selection of Humorous Mess Room Tales

Contents

Dedication

This book is dedicated to all those *National Health Service* (NHS) personnel, including my partner, Aleksandra. I would also like to dedicate this book to all private healthcare professionals and keyworkers in the United Kingdom and around the rest of the globe, who have provided the most professional healthcare to patients throughout the ongoing Coronavirus Pandemic (Covid-19). They're all putting their lives at risk, and sacrificing so much, under the most intense, exhausting and arduous conditions. All those healthcare professionals who have tragically lost their lives, the world is indebted to them and we should salute every single individual hero and heroine. To all those surviving healthcare professionals, private healthcare workers, and lest we forget, the countless keyworkers, I want to say on behalf of the 'rest of us around the globe', *thank you so, so, so much*, we're all so grateful and so, so, so proud of you!

Acknowledgements

I would like to thank professional copy-editor, Kevin O'Byrne (www.aspiringauthors.co.uk). His exceptional editing and proofreading skills, which in my opinion are second to none, and his input and being a sounding board for advice, has enabled me to give the reader an insightful, legible and pleasurable reading experience for a fourth time. I would also like to thank Richard Duszcak (www.cartoonstudio.com) for the cartoon drawings that accompany each anecdote throughout this book.

Prologue

The following selection of humorous tales portrays the 'Lighter Side' of working on 'The Dark Side' of the NHS Ambulance

Service. I must confess, though, that I was party to most, but not all, of the incidents that follow, and so can only confirm that those incidents in which I was 'on scene' genuinely occurred. The remainder I heard second or third hand during downtime with my fellow colleagues in the mess room of various ambulance stations. Those stories I've written as accurately as I can remember them being recited to me, including the dialogue, though I do not profess it to be verbatim.

About the Author

In June 2002, Andy commenced employment with the Mersey Regional Ambulance Service, which later merged with the Cumbria, Greater Manchester and Lancashire Ambulance Services to form the Northwest Ambulance Service NHS Trust. He rapidly progressed from the Patient Transport Service (PTS) to qualified paramedic status via Ambulance Technician Training, experience gained in the job, and further extended training from which, upon qualifying, he was presented with a 'Professional Paramedic Development Award' for most improved candidate. In 2005 he registered with the Health Professions Council (HPC), the national governing body for UK paramedics; this changed its name to the Health and Care Professions Council (HCPC) in August 2012. Andy spent the earlier part of his career working in the English counties of Cheshire and Merseyside. In 2007, after living 'up north' for 32 years, Andy relocated down south with his wife and two children, residing there until he and his family relocated to North Yorkshire in September 2013. There, Andy continued his career as an NHS paramedic with the Yorkshire Ambulance Service until October 2015. Content that he'd enjoyed an incredibly rewarding career, and very proud to have saved many lives and made a significant difference to countless others, Andy decided to 'hang up' his stethoscope and explore other projects. He currently spends his working week doing what he enjoys the most... writing.

If you'd like to read more about the author, and to view a very poignant YouTube video of the training and work of a paramedic, then please visit: **www.andythompson-author.com.**

Foreword

Avid readers of Andy Thompson's books, including tales published in *'The Lighter Side – An NHS Paramedic's Selection of Humorous Mess Room Tales'*, will not be disappointed with this sequel. Andy's dark, bizarre, and in equal measure bonkers and hilarious scenarios that he and his fellow colleagues have attended to, will have you laughing out loud, I'm sure.

Andy has the ability to view and approach life... and death, from the perspective of the unpredictable twists and turns a paramedic working a 12-hour shift often encounters; capturing life's events in a way that all UK frontline ambulance service personnel will be able to relate to.

Andy and I have known each other for a long time now, and have experienced a lot of humorous incidents together, both on and off duty. I recall the very first time we ever worked together; we laughed about the fact we share the same surname, Thompson, and both agreed that 'Thompson and Thompson' sounds like the typical business name of a funeral directors; hence the irony of the outcome for our patient following our first ever treble-nine call working together, which was an unsuccessful cardiac arrest.

Two of the many, many funny incidents that Andy and I were involved in as an ambulance crew are written in this book: the recollections of the aptly titled *'Language Barrier'*, and *'Holey Harness'*. Andy provides an insight into how humour can be observed, and unofficial sign language can be performed, while attending to some patients!

I'm now looking forward to reading the third and final instalment in 'The Lighter Side' series, which Andy has informed me is going to be titled *'The Lighter Side, Part 3 – A Former NHS Paramedic's Selection of Humorous A&E Handovers'*. Andy has included a couple of brief 'tasters' within the first story of this book, under the wholly appropriate title *'A&E Handovers'*.

We don't all possess the same sense of humour, granted; but I do hope you enjoy reading this book as much as I did. I can say with utmost certainty that it gave me several hours of laugh out loud moments, and professional cartoonist Richard Duszcak's wonderfully drawn illustrations add that extra humour at the end of each story.

Graham Thompson BSc (Hons) – Emergency Care Practitioner (ECP)

Introduction

If you haven't read 'The Lighter Side – An NHS Paramedic's Selection of Humorous Mess Room Tales', then I strongly suggest that you do before reading this sequel. For those of you that have, then you may remember that I said the following: 'Laughter is contagious. The sheer sound of someone laughing out loud is far more infectious than any airborne virus or bacterial infection. When laughter is shared, it brings people together and increases joy and happiness. Laughter also produces healthy physical changes in the body, and shields you from the damaging effects of stress and anxiety. That's right, laughter is a powerful medicine for stress. There's nothing that works faster to bring your mind and body back into balance than a flamin' good belly laugh. A good belly laugh also boosts the immune system and increases immune cells and antibodies, thus improving your resistance to infection.

Laughter also triggers the release of endorphins, the body's own natural 'Happy Pill', and protects the heart by improving the function of blood vessels and increasing blood flow, which can help protect you against a heart attack and other cardiovascular problems. With so much influence to heal and renew, the ability to laugh effortlessly, and often, is a fantastic resource for overcoming difficulties, improving your relationships, and supporting physical, mental and emotional health.

More than just respite from unhappiness, discomfort and pain, laughter gives you the power and courage to find a fresh source of optimism. Even in the most demanding of times, a laugh, or even just a smile, can have a huge impact on your overall wellbeing. Greatest of all, this invaluable medicine is not only fun, it's also free!'

The above, in my personal opinion, is and still will be as factual as night follows day, even during the Covid-19 pandemic at the time of publishing this book, to the present day as you're reading this.

The healthcare professionals, who sacrificed so much to help others, kept a sense of humour and laughed out loud, where appropriate, even in the face of the killer virus.

I also previously wrote: 'I decided to write this book to accompany and **conclude** my *The Dark Side – Real Life Accounts of an NHS Paramedic* series'. However, with encouragement from others I decided to write 'The Lighter Side, Part 2' as there were still so many more humorous tales from my experiences, and the experiences of many friends and colleagues from the ambulance stations I worked at.

Furthermore, in 'The Lighter Side' I also stated: 'I would like to add the caveat that if you find any of the following stories insensitive, crude or distasteful, then please accept my sincere apologies.' Likewise, in this book's case, I apologise in advance if any of you find it in any way sick, twisted, insensitive or distasteful. Should that be the case, then before you criticise, judge or condemn ambulance personnel as being insensitive or unprofessional, please bear in mind that the vast majority of healthcare professionals are very caring and compassionate people. At the same time, from the start of their career many, though not all, ambulance personnel tend to gradually develop a dark sense of humour... if they don't already possess it. Possessing a dark sense of humour is not considered insensitive or unprofessional in ambulance service culture. It is simply a coping mechanism, and is usually only revealed away from the eyes and ears of the patient or members of the public in general.

Note from the author: This book was written, produced and edited in the UK where spellings and word usage can vary from the U.S English. The use of quotes in dialogue and other punctuation can also differ.

A&E Handovers

I'm very fond of the elderly, and from my past experience they tend to remain eighteen years old in the mind, regardless of their age, both male and females. The number of times that I've walked into a patient's house and an elderly lady has said, 'Oh, you're a big strapping lad, aren't you?' Being a cheeky chappy, I usually replied with, 'By heck, Petal, if you were thirty years younger, I'd be after you.' It was welcomed humour, and lightened the situation a little.

This first story involves an elderly patient named Doris, who was approximately eighty-six years old. She had fallen and banged her face on the floor. At around 11:30pm, my crewmate, James, and I were dispatched to attend to Doris. She presented with quite a bruised face, with multiple grazes and cuts. So, James and I undertook the appropriate procedures to ensure Doris was fully assessed, before moving her onto the carry-chair and, shortly after, to the ambulance.

She was fine, nothing life-threatening, so upon arrival at A&E I decided to have a little fun with the triage nurse... granted, not for the first time. I knew the nurse well, and we always had a laugh, both on duty and during staff nights out on the club-strip with other paramedics, doctors and nurses. Doris was hard of hearing, so I took advantage of that in a humorous way: I must add, not in an ageist or disability discriminatory way.

As you may be aware, paramedics, being the first people on scene, generally give a handover to a doctor or nurse to explain the history of events, what the patient's vital observations were, and the treatment given to them, etcetera. So, Janet, the nurse, approached me and said,

"Hi, Andy. What have you got for me?" Out of earshot of anybody else, I said,

"Hi, Janet. This is Doris. She's eighty-six years old, and she is hard of hearing."

"OK. Has she had a fall? Her face is very bruised, the poor old dear," she replied.

"Um. That's the obvious assumption, isn't it, with her being eighty-six. However, no, that's not the case," I explained.

"Really? Why, what's happened then?" Janet asked.

"Well," I said with a despairing sigh, "Doris here was caught in bed with her best friend's husband, doing the old rudey-dudey. A bit of the old 'how's your father', you know? Her best friend, Pearl, who is in her nineties, went absolutely mad and knocked ten cans of shite out of Doris." I was keeping a very straight face.

"You're joking!?" Janet exclaimed.

"No, and furthermore, there's another crew bringing Pearl's husband in. Pearl knocked ten cans of shite out of him, too. What are OAPs like these days, hey, Janet? They're worse than the youth of today!" I said, still keeping a straight face.

Janet's face was a picture of shock and, after several seconds or so, James and I couldn't hold our laughter any longer. The look of sheer disgust on Janet's face at my handover's history of events caused us to crumble, and we burst out laughing. Janet laughed out loud too and said,

"Are you taking the piss, Andy? What's really happened?" Still laughing, I replied,

"You were right the first time; she's had a fall. She needs a little TLC in hospital, and social assessment as she lives alone. A full set of observations proved unremarkable." Following that, with a huge smile on her face, Janet punched me on the arm and said, "Put her in cubicle three, you wind-up merchant."

Some weeks later, my crewmate and I brought a drunken eighteen-year-old into A&E. It was about 02:30am. The duty triage nurse, Jayne, was on a night shift, as were we. This particular patient lay on the stretcher with one shoe on his foot and one shoe placed on the stretcher. He'd vomited all over his training shoe and, for some reason – maybe due to the vomit all over it – it wasn't on his foot upon our arrival at his side. Nevertheless, I obviously took it along with us.

On entering A&E, Jayne approached me, "Hi, Andy. What have we got here? A typical drunken teenager?" she asked.

"Yeah, Jayne, but I witnessed something I've never seen before," I said, with concern on my face.

"Why, what's happened?" she asked, straight-faced.

"Well, he vomited in the ambulance—"

"OK," said Jayne, interrupting.

"And he vomited up that shoe," I said, pointing at the sickly-looking trainer next to him on the stretcher. "Funny really, I personally prefer a kebab after a good sesh!"

"Get away, Andy! Put him in cubicle eight," she replied, shaking her head while laughing.

The above are by no means just two isolated cases of humorous handovers. I've given countless similar handovers to my fantastic, professional medical peers, when circumstances have allowed for it. Admittedly, some didn't possess my sense of humour and, therefore, didn't find them funny. But the vast majority did, and importantly they knew I'd have done a professional and thorough assessment of my patient on scene and en route to A&E, and consequently would give them a factual handover moments later.

Force Nine Gales

It was 9am on a cold, extremely windy autumn morning. Naturally, the trees were bare and leaves were scattered all over lawns, the roads, pathways and pavements. My crewmate, Meg, and I were sat on station having a cuppa, discussing observational humour and the like, when our radio handsets sounded.

"Go ahead, over," I said.

"Roger. I'm passing a RED call through to your ambulance monitor now," the dispatcher informed me. Meg and I quickly vacated our seats and proceeded to our vehicle.

The call was to attend to a fifty-six-year-old gentleman experiencing chest pain, though the nature of the call is not significant to this story; it's what happened en route that is... Oh, and very funny!

Try your utmost to visualise this: We were driving along on blue lights and sirens in the direction of the address given to us. As we approached a give-way junction, a lady looked at us and gestured the symbolic Catholic cross; you know, the 'spectacles, testicles, wallet and watch' gesture. After passing the lady, Meg and I couldn't help but laugh out loud. It doesn't end there.

After a further mile or two of driving, a nearer crew became 'clear' (that is, available) and so we were stood down from that incident and diverted to another treble-nine call. Meg did a safe U-turn and began driving back towards the direction we had come from. The religious lady had ambled a little further along the paved roadside by now, and as we passed her, still using blue lights and sirens, she once again gave us the 'spectacles, testicles, wallet and watch' gesture. I assumed she thought we were a different ambulance crew. It doesn't end there.

Typically in the ambulance service, you can be diverted time and time again as treble-nine calls come in, depending on the severity and nature of the call. And so it was that Meg and I were once again stood down and diverted... back in the direction of the religious lady. We were beginning to feel truly blessed as the lady displayed the symbolic gesture to us for a third time as we passed her. But what made this incident even more memorable was not only this seemingly very devout lady, there was also a workman.

This workman was leaf blowing council owned lawns, during what was a day of force nine gales!

He was leaf blowing, but the leaves were just gusting back in his face and across the surrounding area. It was a pointless task, but he continued to do it anyway. Meg and I were in stitches thinking of the lady gesturing the Catholic cross each time we passed her, while a leaf blowing council workman performed his duties, at the tax payers' cost, with absolutely no logic whatsoever.

A Tight Fit

There are times during a shift as an ambulance crew, day or night, when on arrival at the address given, immediate access to a patient, or a patient's property, is not always possible.

Patients sometimes press their 'Lifeline' pendant, worn around their neck like a necklace. In addition to the necklace, there's usually a cord hanging from the bathroom ceiling, too. The patient alerts Lifeline and tells the duty Lifeline Operator that they require an emergency ambulance response. The Lifeline Operator gives ambulance control the code to a key safe at the property, which is then passed onto the crew via the radio. The crew then input the number and retrieve the key to unlock the front door; a very clever idea and, from experience during my career on the frontline, also a very professional and efficient service.

However, not all elderly patients possess a key safe, nor do they all hire the services of Lifeline. In those cases, we would have to simply shout through the letterbox and look to see if we could set eyes on the patient and gauge what condition they were in, and also whether we were able to communicate with them or not. Then, if necessary, we would request the police service to respond with the 'Enforcer' or 'Battering Ram'; in slang terms it's called the 'red key'.

This next incident involves just that circumstance. John, an ambulance technician, and I were dispatched to an address a short distance from the ambulance station. A seventy-odd year-old elderly lady, who lived alone, had fallen but had managed to ring treble-nine herself. She was unable to get up off the floor without assistance as she was in pain, and had informed the ambulance controller that she may have fractured her hip bone – more commonly known as a fractured neck of femur to medical personnel. Upon our arrival, we immediately proceeded down the garden pathway towards the front door. I peered through the letterbox to see if I could spot the patient, but I couldn't.

"Hello, ambulance service. Can you hear me at all?" I shouted.

"Help, help! I'm on the floor! I can't get up!" the lady shouted.

"Just bear with us, we'll get to you, don't worry," I assured her. "What's your name?"

"Gladys!" she shouted back as best she could. I tried the door handle to see if the door just happened to have been left unlocked. It hadn't.

"Right, John, I'm going to request the 'red key'. Keep talking to Gladys through the letterbox."

I contacted ambulance control and asked for the police to attend with said 'key'. A few minutes later, control passed a message to me via my handheld radio, informing me that the police were very busy and a unit with the equipment I'd requested may not become available for up to an hour. John had been listening to the message too, so he began wandering around the back of the house to see if any windows were unlocked or ajar. I, however, continued talking to Gladys through the letterbox, asking various questions and trying to reassure her. Then I heard John shout to me,

"Andy! There's a window open round here!"

"OK mate!" I shouted back to him. "Gladys, keep calm and bear with us. I'm just going to see my crewmate."

I strode round the back of the flat, where John pointed out a small window which was wide open. 'Great,' I thought. However, at a glance it appeared to be quite a small window that probably led to the bathroom, but we wouldn't know until one of us had climbed up and peered inside. I turned to John and said,

"You definitely weigh less than me. What do you weigh?"

"About ten stone, maybe ten and a half," he replied. I grinned at him with pleasure.

"Well, I'm about twelve stone, maybe a touch over," I said with a smug look on my face, "I think it's best that you climb through." With a look of despair on his face, John gave a big sigh, looked up at the window and then agreed to do it. "Come on, John, I'll give you a bunk-up. Just empty your pockets, give me your radio and take your utility belt off."

John stood close to the wall, while I crouched slightly and placed my hand underneath the sole of his left boot. "One, two, three," I said, counting out loud before assisting him up. He grabbed hold of the window frame and I pushed his feet upwards, allowing him to get his head through and his torso to rest on the bottom part of the window frame. "Well done, mate. Is it the bathroom?" I asked.

"Yeah. I'm gonna have to drop into the bath, though," he stated.

"Shit! Don't do it if you think you're gonna get hurt. You can come out if you want, I'll chase up the ETA of the police," I said. I had John's safety in mind, but nevertheless it looked quite funny seeing him hanging half through a window and half out.

Squeezing a little further through the small window, John began resembling a single sardine stuck in a whole tin of the little fish.

"How you doin'? Can you get through any more, at all?" I asked, as he seemed to have just stopped moving.

"Andy..."

"Yeah?" I replied.

"I'm f**kin' stuck, mate," he said while just hanging there, wiggling his legs about.

"What do you mean you're stuck? You're like a shaved sparrow! I've seen more meat on a butcher's knife," I emphasised in a humorous tone and giggling to myself. "Just get your fat arse through the window, you skinny git," I said, stating an obvious contradiction in terms.

"I'm telling you, I'm f**kin' stuck!"

"Right," I said. "Try and wriggle out then. I'll support you down."

"I can't. I'm f**kin' stuck! I'm like Augustus Gloop in the chocolate pipe in Willy Wonka!" he quipped. Well, at that I just burst out laughing.

"I've told you a million times, do not exaggerate," I replied through stifled laughs. John, however, saw no room for laughter at this point; and when I say 'no room for laughter', I mean it literally. I doubt he could have expanded his chest enough to laugh out loud!

I left John hanging out of the window for a moment and went to peer through the letterbox once again, to make sure that Gladys was still OK. After a short chat with her, reassuring her that help was on its way, I returned to John. I gave a few more words of encouragement between the occasional laugh, then heard sirens.

"This could be the police," I said, chuckling to myself, "probably not with the 'red key' but to arrest you on suspicion of attempted burglary." Then I burst out laughing again.

"Just get me out," he said, attempting a chuckle, though a little muted. "I'm f**kin' stuck and it's gettin' f**kin' uncomfortable now." Moments later the police arrived, fortunately with the 'red key' and not because they'd received reports of a burglar.

I explained the rather embarrassing situation to them. Consequently, both police officers couldn't resist first having a look at John stuck in the window, and almost keeled over laughing.

I stood below John and explained to his dangling legs that, following the police gaining access, I was going to see to Gladys first, and then I'd ask them to help him out of the window from both inside and out. The police promptly gained access with the 'red key' and I immediately commenced a thorough assessment of Gladys, occasionally chuckling to myself throughout the process.

Ten minutes later, John entered the lounge where I was seeing to Gladys, appearing extremely relieved that he'd been freed from the bathroom window. We treated Gladys accordingly and conveyed her to A&E.

After handing over Gladys to the triage nurse, we cleared with ambulance control and drove back to the station for a brew. Upon arrival back at 'base', John couldn't resist relaying the recent laughable circumstances of such a tight fit. He had the other staff in the mess room in stitches while listening to the tale, and consequently, for several weeks later, John was addressed by all as Augustus Gloop. Brilliant!

Sixth Sense

I'm not a religious man, but I do uphold Christian values; most of the time, anyway. I also adore churches and I'm fascinated by cemeteries and graveyards. I particularly enjoy reading very old headstones. I don't profess to visit them often, but an occasional walk around a church and/or cemetery can be quite therapeutic. I don't know why, but the peace and tranquillity is great.

This next incident involves a treble-nine call that my lovely crewmate, Izzie, and I attended to, one bleak, autumn Sunday afternoon. It was about three or four o'clock on a dull, miserable, cold day, and dusk was drawing in. We'd had a reasonably quiet nine or ten hours on duty thus far, and had shared a lot of laughs and banter together. I loved working with Izzie, we were a good crew and our shifts together were not only pleasant but often full of both light and dark humour.

I remember, just several days prior to the following incident, Izzie telling me that she'd been to a wedding the previous weekend. She'd explained to me that, during the evening reception, she'd got speaking to a bloke at the bar. During the conversation with him, he asked her what she did for a living. Being a little tipsy at the time, her response to his question was, "I see dead people." Apparently, the bloke was a little taken aback by her answer.

"So, you're an embalmer?" he asked, apparently intrigued, according to Izzie when she explained the conversation to me.

"Oh, no. No," she replied. He then took a second guess at her job title,

"A mortician?" he asked.

"No."

"I give up. Just tell me, please."

"I'm a paramedic," she informed him. The gentleman was amazed, as Izzie was a petite, girly girl type.

"I wouldn't have thought someone your size could manage lifting people down the stairs," he said.

He couldn't have been more wrong. I've worked with a lot of petite female ambulance personnel who could lift heavy patients just as well as their male colleagues could, with no problems whatsoever! Anyway, I slightly digress.

Izzie and I were ambling along in the ambulance when a treble-nine call was passed to us by ambulance control. An elderly lady had fallen whilst walking around the church cemetery on a visit to lay fresh flowers on her late husband's grave.

"Do you know where this church is, Andy?" Izzie asked.

"Yeah, I've attended jobs both inside and outside the church we're heading to, on several occasions. Apparently, it's haunted," I replied.

While mobilising in the direction of the church using blue lights and sirens, Izzie asked, "Is it really supposed to be haunted?"

"Oh yeah, allegedly. I doubt it though," I said with an element of cynicism in my tone.

Within several minutes we'd arrived on scene. We grabbed the appropriate equipment from the saloon of the vehicle and proceeded towards the church gates, where we were beckoned by another lady who was comforting the patient. As we arrived at the patient's side, I introduced both Izzie and I, "Hello. My name's Andy and this is Izzie. What's your name?" I asked the old dear.

"Mavis," she replied.

"Ah, Mavis. What a lovely name. Do you know the meaning of the name Mavis?" I asked.

"No," she replied, looking at me with intrigue.

"The name Mavis means 'Songbird' or 'Song Thrush', and its English origin means joy, loved, strong and fearless. I only know that because my nan's name was Mavis. You see, you learn something every day, even while lying on a church's cemetery grounds," I said with a smile on my face. The Good Samaritan then spoke up.

"She was walking round the grounds, but the lawn is really uneven, and so she lost her footing and fell over. She's in good spirits—"

"Was that pun intended?" I asked, interrupting.

She laughed. "No, no pun intended. She's in good spirits, but I didn't want to move her. I thought it best that I wait for you to arrive. Can I leave her with you, as I have to go? I'm in a rush. In fact, I'm late already," the Good Samaritan explained.

"Yeah, yeah, that's fine. Thank you for staying with her. She'll be fine with us, don't worry."

We crouched down alongside Mavis, Izzie at her head end and me by her side. Izzie began questioning her, while I commenced the task of obtaining some vital observations.

After several minutes had passed, and with Izzie and I being satisfied that Mavis was reasonably comfortable, we made the clinical decision that she had no significant injuries requiring A&E attention. She simply needed assisting to her feet, placing onto the carry-chair and wheeling to the warmth of the ambulance for a few further tests, and to ascertain her social circumstances for welfare reasons, such as whether she lived alone. I also had to find out whether any family could come and drive her home, or if a taxi was the only option.

As we continued to discuss the next plan of action, Izzie began to stare over my shoulder, as if looking behind my back at something.

"What's up, Izzie?" I asked.

"There's a woman over there, gawping at us," she said. "Look, but don't make it obvious." I inconspicuously took a glance over my shoulder and could clearly see a woman. However, possessing the gift of spontaneous wit, I decided to have a little fun at Izzie's expense.

"Where?" I asked, furrowing my eyebrows as if confused.

"Over there, behind you. She's stood next to that headstone." I once again glanced over my shoulder.

"There's nobody there, Izzie. You're seeing things. It's probably the poor light playing tricks on your eyes."

That last remark of mine caused Izzie's face to become a picture of fear and disbelief, no doubt remembering that I'd said the church was allegedly haunted. She continued staring in the direction of the woman, and intermittently glancing at me.

It was proving to be good fun so far, and my mind was doing somersaults on how I could progress this wind-up further. I pondered for a brief moment and then asked,

"Izzie, can you go and get the carry-chair and two blankets, please? I'll stay with Mavis." Izzie then made her way to the ambulance parked on the roadside outside of the church grounds. At the same time, I noticed the gawping woman walk inside the church through a side entrance, which gave me the opportunity to progress the wind-up further.

I leant over Mavis to inform her of what we were going to do. "Mavis, Izzie's gone to get the chair so we can get you off the ground and into the ambulance for further examination. We'll get you in a warmer place. OK?"

"Yes, that's fine, my love," she replied.

16

"While I'm here and we're waiting, I'd just like to take some pictures of the beautiful surroundings of the church. Is that OK with you, Mavis?" I asked. Mavis nodded her approval. So, using my mobile phone camera, I took a picture of where the woman had previously been stood, and also several other pictures of around the grounds, including the main entrance to the church.

When Izzie returned with the carry-chair and blankets, I was crouched back down in my original position next to Mavis. By now, the woman had returned and was stood roughly in the same position she had been a short time earlier, though she wasn't looking at us, merely perusing various headstones it seemed. Then Izzie spoke,

"There's that woman again." I looked over my shoulder once again, and said,

"Where? Who are you referring to, Izzie? I can see a listing headstone that looks a bit like a woman, but it's a headstone. It's just a trick to the eyes, that's all. There's nobody there, hun."

"Are you blind, Andy?! She's stood about twenty feet behind you," Izzie remarked.

At that point I said, "Right, I'll take a picture to prove there's no woman there." I came to my feet, turned to face the area where the lady was stood, and positioned myself to take a photograph. The mobile phone camera clicked. Then I went to the phone's photo gallery and loaded a picture I'd taken while Izzie had been fetching the carry-chair. "There, have a look at that, Izzie," I said as I showed her the picture of the area and headstone where Izzie could see a woman. She carefully focussed her eyes at the screen. Her jaw dropped, she shivered and went chalk white.

"Oh my god, Andy, I'm shitting myself! The hairs are standing up on the back of my neck! What the hell?!"

"Language, Izzie. We're outside a place of worship," I said to remind her, trying hard not to laugh.

We crouched down next to Mavis once again, taking up the same positions as previously, Izzie at the head end and me alongside the elderly patient, facing Izzie. Then I saw Izzie nod her head and give a thumbs up to somebody behind me. I looked over my shoulder and could see the vicar stood there. However, I turned to Izzie and frowned at her, as if confused, and said,

"Who are you giving the thumbs up to?" The vicar had now turned around and begun studying the church, as if weighing up a task or problem that needed some attention or repairs in the future.

"Give over, Andy. It's the vicar. He's just signalled a thumbs up to ask if everything's OK," Izzie said. So, once again I got my mobile phone out and took a picture of the vicar with his back turned to us. An evident click could be heard from my mobile.

"There," I said while showing Izzie another of the pictures I'd captured earlier. "I suppose that proves this place *is* haunted. Never mind, don't worry. Let's get Mavis onto the carry-chair."

As I prepared the carry-chair and blankets, Izzie looked at me, appearing ashen and unsettled; ghostly white in fact. "I feel sick, Andy," she said, quivering. "I'm scared now. Are you winding me up?"

"No, I'm not, but don't worry yourself," I said with a straight face. "Tell me, what did the vicar look like? Was he tall with grey hair and glasses?" I asked.

"Yeah, he was. Why?" Izzie asked, curious but with a fearful look on her face.

"He died three years ago. His headstone is over there somewhere, not sure where exactly," I said out of earshot of Mavis. "The current vicar is quite short and stocky... Oh, and black," I informed her with a very serious look on my face. Izzie's jaw hit the floor once again; not literally, that'd be like a zombie movie!

"Ohhhhh myyyyyy god! I've gone cold, Andy, I feel sick. Please can we get out of here as quickly as possible?"

"Yeah, we're nearly ready. Don't worry, they can't do you any harm. You're obviously gifted, you really can see dead people," I emphasised, attempting to remind her of what she had told the bloke at the wedding reception.

We assisted Mavis to her feet and sat her on the carry-chair, wrapped her up with blankets and wheeled her to the warmth of the ambulance. Following further examination, and Izzie and I being happy that she was safe to go home without a visit to A&E, we waited patiently for Mavis's relative to arrive to drive her home.

On arrival back at the ambulance station, Izzie immediately ran to the toilet. I assumed it was to change what had once been a perfectly good pair of knickers... or to vomit, or both. And maybe to splash some much-needed cold water on her face. Meanwhile, I recited the wind-up to fellow colleagues, and soon had them bent over in stitches.

A short time later, Izzie emerged from the ladies toilet and entered the mess room, still looking ghostly white! All the staff immediately stared at her and burst out laughing.

"You've been 'ad, Izzie!" Mark said.

"What?!" she asked.

"You've been 'spooked'!"

Izzie looked at me for a few seconds, sheer anger on her face. "Andy, you b*****d! I don't believe you! Could you see that woman and the vicar all along?"

"Of course I could. I was winding you up because you told that bloke at the wedding reception that you see dead people," I said between bouts of laughter. The staff in the mess room continued laughing, too.

The story went round various ambulance stations for several weeks. It was a great wind-up to be involved in, and especially to have been the instigator of. The story is typical of the humorous pranks carried out amongst ambulance crews... particularly by the 'old school' paramedics!

You Little...

If you've never had to ring treble-nine to request an emergency ambulance, then you may not know that the ambulance controller has a set script to follow. I don't know the script in detail as I've never worked as a controller, but I do know that they ask the caller to close animals in, particularly dogs, in order for the crew to be safe and undistracted. However, this next incident didn't quite go according to plan.

The emergency wasn't occurring inside the caller's house, it was happening in the street, just outside the house. The lady caller didn't know who the patient was, she had simply witnessed him collapse and promptly called treble-nine. Consequently, she would have felt no reason to close her dogs in a room, even though the controller – despite being informed that the patient was in the street – would have probably told her to close her animals in (following the set script – crazy, I know).

Regardless that the script didn't *really* apply to her, what was about to ensue shortly after my crewmate, Louise, and I arrived on scene, shows it isn't so crazy after all. As we hurriedly ran towards the gentleman's unconscious body, the lady had very little control over what was to happen next.

I rapidly began a speedy airway assessment, while Louise applied the ECG pads. Unfortunately, the patient was in asystolic cardiac arrest; that's a 'flat line' to the layperson. Louise immediately commenced cardiac chest compressions. However, before I even got chance to consider getting the bag-valve-mask (BVM) out to provide artificial ventilations to the patient, two Jack Russells came hurtling from the caller's house.

"Oh shit! They look aggressive," I said to Louise. "Keep doing compressions, though."

Before I knew it, I had one growling, aggressive Jack Russell tugging at my trouser leg, and another jumping on me and practically standing on my back.

"Arrrgh! Get off you little...!" I shouted, doing my utmost to refrain from swearing. Meanwhile, Louise, as she continued lifesaving compressions, couldn't help but laugh because they were leaving her alone. Then out came the owner.

"I'm so sorry. Bonnie, Cheeky! Get in right now!" she shouted. Both dogs completely ignored her, and so I literally crawled, dragging one ankle-biter along the floor, with the other jumping on my back, delaying me from reaching for the BVM so I could commence ventilations to the patient. As the dogs continued to both attack and distract me, I shouted,

"Oh my dog! Can you get these little ankle-biters off me, please, love! We're trying to save a bloody life here, for fluff's sake!" With Louise continuing to laugh, the owner tried once more.

"Bonnie, Cheeky! Get off the man, now!" she once again ordered. "I'm so sorry, they're not normally like this, it must be the uniform," she said, grabbing a hold of their collars and dragging them up the pathway.

"Thank god for that. They're barking mad," I said to Louise while having a moment of laughter, too.

We continued treatment and thought that the ordeal was over, when all of a sudden one of the dogs broke loose from the caller's clutches and ran straight back at me. Whether it was Bonnie or Cheeky I don't know, as I wasn't paying any attention to its sex organs! Once again it began tugging at my already shredded trouser leg. I couldn't help but laugh, as I couldn't believe the situation we were in, trying to work on a cardiac arrest while being attacked by two huge 'rats'. My laughter caused Louise to laugh again, and once more I shouted to the lady, doing my level best not to swear by choosing to change obscenities into dog-related words,

"Fluffing 'ell, love! Can you get this huge rat off me, we're trying to save a life here, for fluff's sake!"

"Bonnie! Bonnie! Get in you little shit! I'm so sorry," she said, once again dragging the dog off me by its collar and pulling it through the front door. 'Finally! The ordeal is over,' I thought. However, Cheeky managed to escape from around the back, and so, a short time after Bonnie had gone, Cheeky was jumping on me and tugging at my trouser leg again.

"Fluffing attack Louise instead, you little—"

"Eh, don't get it on to me. He obviously likes me, but it doesn't like you," Louise retorted.

Once again, the lady scrambled down the pathway, clutched at the 'rat's' collar and dragged him down the garden and inside the house. Speedily continuing with treatment, I asked Louise to get the stretcher from the ambulance, while I undertook one-man basic life support. Minutes later, she emerged with the stretcher, so we quickly lifted the patient in to position and wheeled him into the ambulance. There, we were able to provide advanced resuscitation measures and convey him to hospital under blue light conditions.

After handing over the patient to A&E staff, we returned to the station. When we entered the mess room, our colleagues stood open mouthed in sheer surprise at what they saw.

"What the hell has happened to you, Andy?! You've got dirty... what is that, they look like paw prints all over your back? And your trouser leg is ripped to shreds. What happened?" Louise and I glanced at each other and just burst out laughing.

"Don't ask," I said, shaking my head, "you wouldn't believe me if I told you!"

Fortunately, the A&E staff continued resuscitation to great success. I'm led to believe the patient responded well to treatment, made a good recovery and was eventually discharged from hospital with only mild disabilities... by some miracle, that is!

Fire Service, Please

Am I right in saying that, at some point in our personal relationships and intimate sex lives, most of us have tried, one way or another, role play, sexual experimentation, etcetera? Yes, no? There's nothing to be ashamed of, it's perfectly normal and healthy. This next incident involves just that - sexual experimentation with domination – that went embarrassingly wrong.

Adam, an ambulance technician, and I were in the ambulance under normal driving conditions, when we were dispatched to a thirty-year-old female having an anxiety attack. They're usually straightforward incidents to deal with, particularly in those under fifty years old. However, what we were going to be presented with on our arrival was not so common. In fact, I'd never dealt with it before and I never dealt with the same situation ever again during the rest of my career.

Upon arrival at the address given, I noticed that the door was ajar, so we wandered inside. "Hello, ambulance service!" I shouted. A man, aged about thirty to thirty-five, was stood at the top of the stairs, dressed only in his underwear. He beckoned us to go upstairs, so with equipment in our possession, we ambled up the staircase.

Now, it might be a good time to point out to you that, hanging on the newel post at the bottom of the stairs, was a hi-visibility jacket emblazoned with a reflective *'POLICE'* badge across the back. I could only assume that either the gentleman, or the lady we had been called to attend to, was a police officer.

When we arrived outside the bedroom, the gentleman blocked our access. He had something to explain prior to allowing us entry.

"Look, guys, this is a really embarrassing situation for us both. Before you go in, can you please promise you won't laugh or tell anybody else?" he asked, his cheeks rather flush.

"Yeah, that's fine, pal, what's the problem?" I asked. "There's nothing embarrassing about having a panic attack." But as I said it, a gut feeling stirred in my stomach and I anticipated something funny was on the opposite side of the door.

We entered the bedroom and, not to our surprise, found the young lady, our patient, lying on the bed, practically naked... oh, and each of her wrists separately cuffed to the metal headboard. She wasn't only having a panic attack, she was sweating and was very red-faced, too.

"Why haven't you covered her dignity before we got here?" I asked, frowning.

"I did, but she keeps kicking the duvet off because she's panicking," he replied. 'Acceptable answer,' I thought.

"OK. What's her name, and does she normally have panic attacks, or is it the situation she's panicking about?" I asked him, with relevance.

"Her name's Lisa. No, she doesn't normally. It's the embarrassing situation that's causing it," he replied. Adam promptly covered Lisa with the duvet, but once again she kicked it off while expressing that she didn't want the duvet on her. Adam immediately began reassuring her and then started coaching her breathing to try and restore it to a normal respiratory rate. Fortunately, Lisa wasn't experiencing any carpo-pedal spasm. Had she been, it would have caused severe pain in the wrists, particularly while wearing the handcuffs, and her distress would have been elevated even further.

"Why can't you unlock her? Where's the keys?" I asked with obvious relevance.

"She told me where they should be, but they're not there. I can't find them anywhere," he said, once again despairing. 'Oh dear,' I thought, 'this is only going to get more embarrassing.'

"Right, Adam, keep coaching her breathing and get a set of observations when you can," I said. I then turned to the gent. "I'm really sorry but I'm gonna have to get the fire service out. They've got the right equipment to free her from the handcuffs." The gent covered his face with both open palms, as if in despair. After a few seconds, he dragged his hands down across his cheeks and then looked at me again.

"I thought you guys would carry something that'd cut cuffs off. Surely?" he said, perhaps more in desperate hope than truly believing paramedics would arrive equipped with metal cutters.

"No, sorry... no. Why are you so concerned, there's no need to be?" I asked, somewhat intrigued at the desperation in his voice. He just began to shake his head.

"They're gonna take the piss out of me indefinitely," he said.

"Who is?" I asked.

"The lads from the station."

I began putting two and two together and it was adding up to four. "You're a police officer?" I asked, trying not to laugh.

"No," he replied. 'Oh,' I thought, 'not what I was taught in school then, two and two must add up to five.'

"So is Lisa a copper then, and you're a firefighter?"

"Yeah, she's a special constable, and the lads all know Lisa," he emphasised with a huge sigh. "That's why we used her cuffs. She's not done her rigid cuff training yet, so she only has two sets of the old style," he explained.

The situation wasn't going to get any better anytime soon. I contacted ambulance control to request the fire service to attend, briefly explaining that our patient was in a somewhat compromising position, and that we required cutting equipment ASAFP.

While we waited patiently for the arrival of the fire service, Adam continued coaching Lisa's breathing, and after several minutes he had managed to calm her down considerably. He also undertook *some* vital observations, which proved normal under the circumstances. Moments later, we saw blue flashing lights bounce off the bedroom window. It was 'the cavalry', who possessed the equipment needed to free this red-faced special constable.

"Hello! Fire service!" a man shouted from the bottom of the stairs. To save them both from too much further embarrassment, I left the bedroom to meet the fire officer in charge. I briefly informed him of the situation, and also explained that we didn't need every team member of the *station watch* in the bedroom; just one or two of them with the appropriate cutting equipment would suffice.

Following my explanation, the fire officer and I entered the bedroom. He recognised both of them immediately.

"Hello, Nick. Hello, Lisa," he said with a huge grin on his face. Both Nick and Lisa's faces turned a shade of fresh red!

"Hi, gov," Nick said, frantically rubbing his face with open palms. Lisa, on the other hand, said nothing, even though she was now a lot calmer.

"Right," said the officer, "I'll get *one*," he said with emphasis, "just *one* of the lads to bring the hydraulic pedal cutter and bolt cutter in. The rest of the lads will stay outside. OK?"

"Yeah. Cheers, chief," Nick replied, with a sense of relief in his tone. The fire officer left the room and proceeded to the fire appliance.

I don't know exactly what he said to the lads stood outside, but when I looked through the bedroom window, I witnessed them all bent over laughing. I grinned and thought to myself, 'I won't say anything as it may cause Lisa to start panicking again.' While it was funny, I didn't want that to happen. Minutes later, a fireman arrived in the bedroom with equipment to hand.

"Hi, Nick. Hi, Lisa. You randy devils, what've you been up to?" he asked with an unconcealed smirk on his face, poorly attempting to hide the need to laugh.

"Don't take the piss, John, just get on with it," Nick said, his embarrassment obvious in his voice.

As I, the fire officer and Adam looked on, John started the small hydraulic machine up. The sound of the pedal cutter resonated round the room as he started cutting through the first handcuff, switching to the bolt cutters to complete the cut. A short time later, he began cutting through the second handcuff, again completing the task with bolt cutters. Lisa was finally free! She jumped out of the bed with just her knickers on, and hastily ran straight to the bathroom, slamming the door shut.

"Cheers, John," I said, "much appreciated." Then Nick left the room too. We all glanced at each other, trying to make as little noise as possible, but then all burst out laughing. It was needed; I'd been holding my laughter in for so long that it was beginning to hurt. The release of a good old belly laugh was a relief.

So, if you're thinking of firing things up in the bedroom, particularly with handcuffs, take this story as a word of warning: always have the keys to hand *before* you actually handcuff your partner to the headboard – or anywhere else for that matter.

Oh, just a second word of warning: it's not just police handcuffs that have keys. Even pink, fluffy handcuffs come with keys, too!

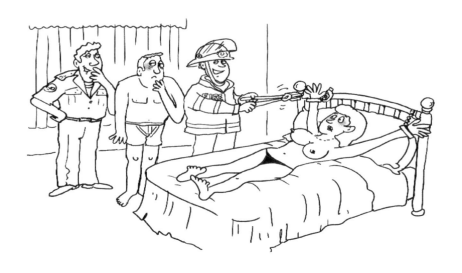

Up and Over

This next incident, though it could have proved to have had a life-changing or even a tragic ending, actually concluded well and thus provided a humorous anecdote that I can share with you.

As you may all be aware, ambulance service personnel frequently deal with patients who have had a little too many 'sherbets', shall we say. This next incident involved two women, both approximately twenty-five years old, who had done just that. Their Friday night of frivolity ended a little unfortunately for one of them. I call it 'bad karma'. The patient called it downright dangerous and criminal! Allow me to explain.

James and I were on a nightshift during the summer season. It was close to midnight and we'd already dealt with several intoxicated individuals thus far. A short time after midnight, ambulance control received a call from the door supervisor of a popular nightclub, stating that a woman was outside on the floor, lying in her own vomit. With James and I being the nearest crew available, we were dispatched to attend.

On our arrival at the nightclub, we immediately spotted a reveller laid on the top step of the doorway, being 'baby sat' by the bouncer. Alongside the patient was her friend, who was still standing but evidently intoxicated too. We vacated the ambulance and approached the patient.

I immediately crouched down and began a primary assessment, leaving the bouncer to continue with his door supervising duties. The ambulance was only several feet away, near the club entrance. After being satisfied that the patient could be assisted to her feet, she staggered, with our underarm support, to the side door of the ambulance, stumbled into the saloon and dropped herself onto the passenger/patient seat. Her drunken friend boarded the ambulance too, but remained stood.

Due to it being a warm summer's night, and not conscious of any confidentiality concerns, I decided to leave the side door open to allow some fresh air in. James commenced some vital observations, while I tried to rouse the patient and gain some information.

"What's your name?" I asked.

"H-h-her n-name's Sue," her friend replied, swaying a little.

"Thank you, but I'd rather her try and answer for herself," I replied.

"A-are, are you takin' her to f**kin' hospickle or w-what?" she asked with an obnoxious tone, albeit slurred.

"We're still assessing her. She may not need to yet, or even want to for that matter," I said with some assertiveness in my voice.

"W-well I think s-she f-f**kin' needs to," the reveller replied with a disagreeable tone.

Several minutes passed by and Sue began rousing a little. The observations that James had obtained were completely normal, and we had no concerns whatsoever. Sue's eyes were intermittently opening and closing, but she was able to slur some speech to me.

"I-I d-don't want to go to 'ospital. I j-just want to g-go to bed," she slurred. James began penning her details, that I'd managed to ascertain while questioning her, onto the patient report form. It was looking like she'd be on her way soon, preferably by taxi. I intended to point her in the direction of the nearest taxi rank, which was approximately fifty yards away from the nightclub. However, her friend had other ideas.

"She needs to go to f-f**kin' hospickle, you d**khead, f-f**kin' prick!" she said, using language of the guttersnipe. Just as I was about to respond to her obscene comment, a young lad, about twenty years old, appeared at the open side door. He initially appeared as a drunken nosey-parker, but very quickly recognised James.

"Hiya, mate! You saved my f**kin' life, you did!" he said with certainty. James initially frowned in confusion but then recognised him.

"Hello, buddy. How are you?"

"I'm f**kin' good, thanks to—"

"You're takin' her to f**kin' hospickle, you f-f**kin' d**khead!" she said, her aggressive tone interrupting the young lad. He wandered off and went to have a drunken chat with the bouncers. Meanwhile, bigmouth continued. "F**kin' take us now, or else I'll f-f**kin' knock you both out!"

What I thought and what I replied with were very different. What I thought was, 'You wouldn't stand a chance of knocking either of us out.' However, what I responded with to her threat was, "You're such a classy woman, aren't you... where have you been all my life? You're my dream wife. You're such a good catch."

I probably shouldn't have said that, as it re-lit the fire of fury.

"You f**kin' sarcastic, cheeky b*****d!" she shouted.

"No, I'm not being sarcastic. I really mean it. I'd love to take you home to meet my parents, they'd be so proud of me to date a lovely, well-educated, well-spoken woman like you, and you have such a diverse vocabulary."

James chuckled to himself as he continued completing the paperwork, while calmly conversing with Sue. Once again, bigmouth had another rant at me, only this time in earshot of the young lad whose life James had saved. As we continued to exchange heated and sarcastic responses, the young lad came hurtling over to the ambulance side door, looking quite angry.

"Oi! Bitch! Treat these guys with some respect! They do a great job, and he saved my f**kin' life," he said, pointing at James. "Who the f**k d'ya think you are, kickin' off on these two? You f**kin' stupid, fat bitch!" he exclaimed with sheer anger in his voice. At this point I stepped in and said,

"Don't worry, pal, we'll sort it. Thank you. Just be on your way, OK?" He began walking away but made sure he had the last word.

"You f**kin' ugly, fat bitch. F**kin' watch your f**kin' back!"

James then informed me that his paperwork was complete, and that Sue was free to leave the ambulance. 'Cool,' I thought. Both girls stepped off the ambulance and began walking in the opposite direction, away from the taxi rank. "Girls, girls!" I shouted, "Taxis are that way," I said, pointing in the other direction.

My helpful information was responded to with a two-fingered gesture and "F**k off, you f**kin' prick!" James and I just laughed at bigmouth. We then placed the equipment away ready for the next call, and got back into the front of the ambulance.

Just prior to informing ambulance control that we were clear, I asked James who the young lad was, and what incident he was referring to where he'd saved his life. James explained to me that he had been working solo on a rapid response vehicle (RRV) one Saturday night, when he was called to a young lad who had been stabbed. He'd been a customer inside a kebab shop. Later, an A&E doctor had told James that, had he not arrived so quickly and administered the appropriate treatment that he had, the lad would have died without a doubt. It was understandable the lad was so infuriated; he must have felt he owed James a lot, I suppose.

Anyway, we watched both girls stagger up the hill towards the canal bridge. This, as already mentioned, was in the complete opposite direction of the taxi rank, and also the wrong direction relative to the home address that James had recorded on the PRF. There obviously could have been reasons why she chose not to stay at her home address that night; it wasn't our problem, our duty of care was done... for now, anyway!

After clearing with control, we were asked to return to station for a well-earned brew. James began driving slowly up the hill towards the canal bridge. As we approached the bridge, we could see bigmouth and the young lad arguing.

"Shall we pull over and see what's happening, Andy?" James asked.

"Yeah, I think we better had," I replied. But before we even had chance to put our feet on the tarmac, the lad had grabbed bigmouth in a bear hug grip and thrown her up and over the canal bridge! It was a drop of fifteen to twenty feet into shallow water! We heard a loud scream from her as he let go, and as he did, he shouted,

"Let that be a lesson to you! He saved my life!"

James and I couldn't believe what we had just witnessed. "What the fffffff," I uttered in disbelief. We quickly ran across and leant over the bridge, only to find bigmouth wading through the water towards the canal's edge. We didn't even get chance to say anything to the lad, because he ran off back in the direction of the nightclub.

James and I ran down the steps to help bigmouth climb out of the filthy water. I won't go into the treatment that we provided. Let's just say that, due to the mechanism of potential injuries, we had to fully immobilise her and put in a pre-alert call to A&E. Ironically, our initial patient had become the bedside friend, while the friend had become the patient. Karma? Criminal? Or both? You decide.

What happened to the lad I don't know, I never did see him again. Bigmouth, however, was discharged several hours later with no significant injuries.

Both girls left the hospital completely sober. Though apparently, according to the night duty nurses, bigmouth was a little red-faced, since she had to clamber into a taxi wearing disposable hospital knickers and a hospital gown, while carrying a bag of filthy, wet clothes. Oops!

The Simpsons

You'd be surprised how many people decide that their driveway or pathway needs brushing when an ambulance rolls up nearby their home. Some people ask if everything's OK, while others are just blatantly nosey neighbours who can't bear to miss a thing. Mrs Mangle, a character from the Australian soap opera, *Neighbours*, springs to mind. Blimey, I'm showing my age now!

In addition to nosey neighbours, there's the curiosity of children. There's been many a time when children have run over to my crewmate and I, upon us arriving outside an address, and reeled off questions that they wanted answering. This next story involves just that, but I may have gone a step too far in the name of humour.

Darren, a paramedic, and I were dispatched to attend to an elderly lady complaining of abdominal pain, one Saturday afternoon. We were soon on scene and Darren began questioning and assessing the woman. After several minutes, he asked if I could fetch the drugs bag from the ambulance, as he wanted to administer some analgesia to the old dear.

As I stepped outside and exited through the garden gate, I was met by several children, aged about five or six years old, sat on their bicycles. I brushed past them and stepped into the ambulance, picked up the drugs bag and retraced my steps back towards the gate. As I did, I was asked by one of the children,

"What's 'appened, mate?"

"Erm, well—"

"Is she dead, mate?" another kid asked, interrupting me. In the mood for a little banter with the kids, I replied,

"Do you kids watch The Simpsons, at all?"

"Yeah, it's brill. I love it!" one kid replied. The others all replied indistinctly, as they were talking over one another, but I heard words to the effect of 'yeah, I love it, mate!'

"Well," I said with a huge sigh, "the old lady that lives here loves The Simpsons too. She found the episode that she was watching so funny that she laughed her head off! Can you believe it?! Literally laughed her head off, and her head rolled along the floor!"

"Whoa, that's mad, man! That's so funny," one kid said. As I raised my eyebrows at his response, another little lad asked,

"What's in the bag, mate?"

Holding the bag up and giving it a gentle tap, I replied, "This, sunshine... is my sewing kit. I'm going back into her house now, and I'm going to sew her head back on."

"Whoa! I wanna be an ambulance man one day, if that's what you get to do," the little lad said.

As I smiled and worked my way back down the path to the house, the youngsters cycled away. As they did, I heard one of the kids shout,

"Daaaaad! You're never gonna guess what's 'appened to Mrs Braithwaite!"

Closing the door behind me, I thought, 'Doh! I'll await an impending call to the station manager's office.'

Several weeks went by. I'd expected to receive a written complaint from one or more disgruntled parent but, fortunately, no complaints were ever reported. Phew! I do still wonder, though, if those kids were more than a little intrigued to see the amazingly neat sewing job I'd done on Mrs Braithwaite's neck!

Walter Mitty, Gets Shitty

One of the best aspects during the role of being an employee of the NHS Ambulance Service, particularly for those on the frontline, is the variety of different people that you meet and attend to. Although I'm now a *former* NHS employee, during my career I met some incredible people with fascinating stories to tell, both happy stories and some very sad stories, too. I say *stories* because they were believable. However, I occasionally attended to those of the delusional ilk that got off on telling fallacies; more precisely, sheer BULLSHIT! This next incident not only had me chuckling to myself while questioning the patient, but things also became a little heated and hostile.

Mick, a rookie technician, and I were dispatched to a huge shopping centre that housed quite a large gambling arcade. The arcade was absolutely full of Tipping Point type machines, one-arm bandits, horse racing, motorcycle and car racing games, etcetera. Not my cup of tea but very popular back in 'the day' during the decade this incident occurred.

The description of the patient given to ambulance control by the treble-nine caller, then passed to us via handheld radio, was: a scruffy man, about sixty years old, lay drunk – or asleep – against a one-arm bandit machine. Security had been called to escort him from the premises but they couldn't rouse him and, therefore, called for an ambulance. So Mick and I ambled our way through the shopping centre with our equipment, including the carry-chair on the assumption that our patient may be in no fit state to walk unassisted.

Following a ten-minute walk with a little window shopping while on the move, we arrived inside the arcade. A security guard then kindly escorted us to the patient's 'resting' place. Straightaway, we could see that he'd evidently visited a few 'watering holes' that day, and had drank quite a few 'sherbets'. At first glance he appeared to be carrying an arm injury, and it seemed an x-ray would be prudent.

Despite his demeanour, my conscience and moral ethics would not allow me to judge the man as simply under the influence of alcohol; he may well have had an underlying condition that needed prompt attention, not just a 'drunk' with an arm injury.

Now, I'm not going to go into detail about our clinical assessment or treatment of the patient. What I will say, though, is that following a further ten-minute walk through the shopping centre, with the patient sat on the carry-chair, and some further questioning and conversation with him, I reached a secondary, or more accurately, differential diagnosis very quickly!

Literally within minutes of arriving back at the ambulance and assisting him onto the stretcher, my diagnosis was that he was a Walter Mitty. By that I mean a fantasist, full of unconvincing bullshit! A daydreamer, to give him a kinder description if you like. I'll explain to the best that my memory will serve me, though it may be quite brief. You may also find it a bit difficult to follow unless, that is, you happen to be well versed in any of the armed forces, or are serving or ex-military personnel. If so then you'll probably find it even funnier than those who are neither.

Rewind ten minutes. During our walk through the shopping centre, Tony, our patient, was very eager to inform us that he was ex-Special Air Service (SAS). 'Here we go, there's always one! A wannabe,' I thought. There's more than one delusional 'Walter Mitty' who claims to be ex-SAS. I'd not even remotely enquired about his past job, career or whether he was ex-military, he just blurted it out. Straightaway, I knew this was going to be a fun-filled drive to A&E, not least because I happen to be something of a military enthusiast. I'd read many, many books written by genuine ex-SAS soldiers, so my knowledge of the SAS, while not thorough - having not actually served - was really pretty good.

Tony was under the influence of alcohol, but I wouldn't define him as 'drunk', per se. He was able to distinctly converse with us from the moment that we'd arrived by his side.

Following secondary observations, Mick commenced the ten-mile journey to hospital. Meanwhile, I began completing my PRF, noting down Tony's past medical history, prescribed medications, and so on and so forth. That's when the fun conversation started, when Tony piped up,

"Did I mention that I was in the SAS?" Raising my head briefly to look at him, while concentrating on writing the particulars on the PRF, I said,

"Yes, you did. 'The Regiment' hey! Brilliant, well done!" I did nothing to hide the sarcasm in my tone.

"Yeah, yeah, 'The Regiment'. You won't remember the 'Embassy Siege' will you, you're too young? Well, I should have been there, but I was on leave," he said.

He was right, I was only four years old at the time of the Iranian Embassy Siege. However, I wasn't going to let my age, at the time of such a notorious historical event, stop me from testing his knowledge in order to gauge whether he was genuinely telling the truth. So, I put my pen and clipboard down. 'Right, here we go... your starter for ten,' I thought.

"So, Tony, what squadron were you in whilst in 'The Regiment'?" I asked with relevance, using my index and middle fingers to emphasise quotation marks. He glanced at me, and with a brief pause he replied,

"There's no squadrons. Once you're in Twenty-Two Reg., that's it, you're in," he stated with certainty.

"Oh, right. I thought there were four squadrons that rotate special project duties on a six-month basis," I said. "Wasn't it the vast majority of 'B' Squadron that stormed the embassy? I'm sure it was.

They had to take some from 'A' and 'D' Squadrons too, to bring the numbers up, as some of 'B' Squadron were overseas, training." I was ninety-five percent confident in the accuracy of it, thanks to my 'vast knowledge' of the SAS!

He looked at me with a little surprise on his face, but then continued to attempt to convince me he was 'IT', 'the man', 'the best there was' during his past military service.

"That'd all changed by the time I joined. Squadrons were disbanded, so once you passed selection, you were in the regiment. Full-stop!" he emphasised. I knew he was slowly digging a deeper hole for himself.

You may be asking yourself, why did it matter to me to catch this bloke out, to expose his Walter Mitty traits? Simple. I can't tolerate people who claim to be ex-SAS for the kudos and to satisfy their vanity, and especially when they clearly don't even possess the knowledge to support their claim. Never mind that they haven't actually pushed themselves to the absolute limit needed to genuinely earn the sand beret with winged dagger cap badge displaying the motto *'Who Dares Wins'*. It infuriates me. An acquaintance of mine is ex-SAS, and I know it would infuriate him, too.

I continued probing around the subject matter. "So, Tony. Tell me, had you not been on annual leave during the embassy siege, what weapon would you have used to assault the enemy? What weapons did they use to storm Princes Gate?" I asked. To my disbelief, he gave the most ridiculous answer possible.

"The SA80," he replied.

Well, I couldn't believe what I'd heard, and couldn't resist chuckling to myself. By now I knew this guy hadn't done his homework, which was especially short-sighted if he intended to spend the rest of his life trying to convince people he was ex-Regiment. So much for gaining any respect or kudos. I should have left it there... but I just couldn't.

"Ah, right, the SA80. With or without the SUSAT sight?" I asked, strongly believing that he wouldn't have a clue what a *'SUSAT'* sight was.

"SUSAT sight? Yeah, yeah. It's a good sight," he said. I started tapping my fingers against my forehead as if I was trying to recall something.

"I can't remember now what SUSAT is the abbreviation of. It's on the tip of my tongue. Oh, what is it?" I asked, thinking out loud. He paused for a moment before replying with,

"I can't tell you. It's a secret."

"No, no, it's not a secret! I've got it. It's Sight Unit Small Arms Trilux... SUSAT. Yeah, that's it," I accurately confirmed. He stared at me, a little red-faced. I was still only warming up but we weren't that far from arriving at the hospital, so I picked up my clipboard and continued completing some further details.

While documenting the history of events, I looked at his personal details that I'd hand-written on the PRF. I pondered for a moment, shook my head and then chuckled to myself once again. Something hadn't initially dawned on me, but it had now. But I'd come back to that. For now I continued,

"You know what, Tony, I don't think the SAS did use the SA80 during the siege. It's an assault rifle. It just wouldn't have been adequate for close-quarter combat. I think they were equipped with Heckler and Koch Maglite MP5 machine guns. Now that weapon is ideal for close-quarter combat." Tony began getting fidgety. "I think they were also armed with Remington 870 pump-action shotguns, CS gas and stun grenades, nine-millimetre Browning high-power pistols," I glanced at him, "to name but some of their armoury."

Tony became a little agitated, probably by now aware that I didn't believe he was ex-SAS, and that he'd met his match when it came to the facts about the embassy siege.

"Listen, mate, you're wrong! I was in the SAS, I know what they used! How old were you when the siege occurred? Were you even born?" he asked with some hostility in his voice.

"Oh, I was born, yeah. I was only four at the time though, but I'm an SAS enthusiast and an avid reader of SAS books. I've read books written by Lofty Wiseman, Sir Peter de la Billière, Andy McNab, Chris Ryan, and many, many more. So, although I was only four years old at the time, I've read a lot about the 1980 Embassy Siege," I said, with a slight grin on my face.

"Well, you need to read more, 'cause you're wrong!" he exclaimed with a real edge to his voice.

"Did you know Rusty Firmin or John McAleese, at all, Tony?" I asked.

"No," he replied. Once again, I had a little giggle to myself.

"They were both involved in the storming of the Iranian Embassy," I stated. Tony simply bowed his head and remained quiet for a while.

We were by now approaching the grounds of the hospital and so I thought it would be an appropriate moment to point out to Tony what had only recently dawned on me.

"Tony, something's confusing me here. Something that doesn't add up," I said. "You stated that you're ex-SAS and that you were on leave during the embassy siege, correct?"

"Yeah, that's right," he replied. "Why?"

"Well, the date of birth that you gave me, 1963, would have made you seventeen years old during the siege. You wouldn't have even been able to apply for the SAS at that age. I think you've been telling me porkies, haven't you?"

"No, I f**kin' 'aven't!" he exclaimed aggressively. "I was *in* the SAS!"

"The security guard described you as about sixty years old, but you're obviously much younger than that, aren't you?" I emphasised to him.

"I said I was born in 1953, actually, not 1963!"

"Ah well, your medical records should confirm your date of birth for you, if you're a little unsure," I said. "You know what, Tony, it's those who say they're ex-SAS that are usually wannabes, and have never even been a soldier in a regular regiment, let alone the SAS. If you're in the SAS, or even ex-SAS, I wouldn't go around blurting it out to any Tom, Dick or Harry. If I was SAS or ex-SAS, I wouldn't even tell Mrs Miggins," I said with a little titter.

I expected him to ask who Mrs Miggins was, but he didn't. Instead he told me to f**k off, and then folded his arms in a huff, causing him to grimace as he'd forgotten he was carrying the arm injury. He then remained mute, sulking, causing me to grin to myself.

We rolled up under the canopy of the ambulance parking bays at A&E, and Mick opened the back doors. Tony hastily jumped out, looking rather moody, and stormed – pardon the pun – through the A&E entrance, leaving me and Mick following closely behind him. Mick escorted him to the waiting area, while I went to book Tony in at reception and give my handover to the triage nurse.

My handover went something like this: "Waiting in reception for you is Tony. He's between forty-five and sixty years old, depending on whether he wants to convince you or not that he should've been involved in the 1980 Iranian Embassy Siege in Princes Gate, London. He has had some alcohol and has an arm injury, possibly from collapsing in the arcade. It may require an x-ray. Two sets of vital observations are all within normal parameters. I have no

46

concerns, but if there's any test you can undertake to make an absolute diagnosis of Walter Mitty-itis, then that'd be great. Thank you," I explained. The triage nurse looked at me, rather confused but with a grin on her face.

"What do you mean?" she asked.

"You'll soon find out, I'm sure. Don't believe a word of it, though. He's full of bullshit!" I said, before vacating the ward and exiting the hospital, chuckling.

Bull-shitters, hey! I don't get it. I've known people to claim to be ex-Parachute Regiment, who were too scared to even do a parachute jump for charity. I've also known people to claim to be NHS paramedics, firefighters, nurses or coastguards, in their social media or online dating profiles; I believe that's called 'catfishing'. In other circumstances, too, such as job applications and interviews, and whether male or female.

If they want to carry any of those titles, or that of some other vocational career, then why don't they make the effort to tackle the intense, sometimes arduous training that comes with it, and *earn* the right to the job title and so feel good to be genuinely telling the truth during a conversation? The mind boggles!

Really?!

I remember this next incident being recited to me by a former colleague of mine while we were driving back to the ambulance station from a particularly 'bloody' job, shall we say. It prompted him to tell me a funny tale of a call he'd attended to with his female crewmate, Gemma. I can't remember every exact detail, but as best as my memory will serve me, here we go.

Double paramedic crew, Michael and Gemma, were dispatched to a treble-nine call passed to them, via ambulance control, as a cardiac arrest. Upon their arrival, they entered the house through the back door, which led to the kitchen. It became immediately apparent to them that the patient had been deceased for some considerable time – two to three hours at the very least – and so no clinical intervention was deemed appropriate, hopeful or ethical. The daughter explained to Michael and Gemma that she visited him daily, and on this particular visit had found him lying on the kitchen floor, obviously deceased. Rigor-mortis had already begun setting in.

Without the need to evaluate the situation or surroundings, it was clear the patient had lost a lot of blood. The kitchen was absolutely covered in blood. There was dry, congealed blood on the floor that had pooled from the patient's mouth. There were blood-stained hand, foot and knee prints all over the tiled kitchen floor, and blood all over the tiled walls and the kitchen door, units and work surface. It was like an abattoir.

Given what they were initially presented with, they decided to go upstairs and try to gather some clinical reason for the patient's unexpected death. As they walked through the hallway, they noticed similar signs of blood-stained hand and foot prints on the walls and carpets, along with blood-stained knee prints on the carpeted floor.

Arriving at the top of the stairs, blood-stained hand prints were sporadically found on the walls of the landing. When they entered the patient's bedroom, they discovered evidence of blood-stained bed clothing; it was all over the pillow, bottom sheet and duvet cover. As they followed the trail of blood, they noticed blood-stained prints on the bedroom walls and the bedroom door. It became apparent to them that what had befallen this poor chap looked like haematemesis – that simply means 'vomiting blood'.

Now that you have an understanding of what likely occurred, I'll continue with this humorous mess room tale. 'That's humorous?!' I hear you ask. Well, bear with me on this.

Michael and Gemma worked their way back from the bedroom towards the landing and began walking down the stairs, quietly discussing what they believed had occurred. They both strongly felt that the patient had experienced a sudden onset of severe haematemesis. The root cause was unknown, and was also irrelevant at this point; since it was an unexpected death, a post-mortem examination would be required.

As the two continued into the kitchen to liaise with the patient's daughter, Michael began completing the appropriate documentation. He also contacted ambulance control to request the police, and to notify the man's GP surgery of the unexpected death of one of their patients. While he was doing that, he heard Gemma talking to the patient's devastated, yet very calm daughter. What he heard caused him to raise his eyebrows and have to hold back his laughter.

Gemma very reassuringly said to the daughter of the deceased, "I'm very sorry for your loss today. Please accept our sincere condolences. And if it's any consolation, it doesn't look like he suffered."

While Michael was reciting this to me, I just burst out laughing. "What did you say or do when you heard that?" I asked him.

"I just looked at her with raised eyebrows and thought *really*?! Are you having a laugh?! Didn't suffer?!"

After the police had arrived and all the documentation was complete, Michael and Gemma offered their condolences once again and vacated the property. Now seated in the front of the ambulance, Michael said to Gemma,

"'If it's any consolation, it doesn't look like he suffered'! Did you actually see the blood all over the place?! It looked like he'd staggered while vomiting a torrent of blood, banged into the wall, crawled from his bedroom, banged into the walls along the landing, crawled down the stairs in utter distress, through the hallway and into the kitchen. He must have been absolutely panic-stricken and in agony, and you said to her 'it doesn't look like he suffered'!"

Gemma let out a gentle sigh, raised her eyes to the roof of the cab momentarily, glanced back at Michael and, with a slight grin on her face, replied,

"Well, I was just trying to give her some peace of mind."

Pun Intended!

In the medical profession there are three forms of analgesia used by healthcare professionals: positional, pharmacological, and distractional. An example of 'positional' is drawing the knees towards the chest to reduce abdominal pain. Pharmacological analgesia involves the use of over-the-counter medicines, such as Paracetamol, or prescription-only and controlled medicines, such as codeine and IV morphine.

Distractional analgesia, as the name suggests, involves the healthcare professional in distracting the suffering patient in one of a number of ways, though this form *usually* only works on young children. For example, inflating a protective nitrile glove so that the five fingers resemble the comb and points found on the top of a chicken's head. Once the glove is inflated and tied off, a face is drawn on the ballooned body of the glove, which is then handed to the child who in *most* cases finds it very funny, therefore taking their mind off the pain. Brilliant!

As I said, distractional analgesia works best on young children. However, there have been a fair number of incidences where my crewmate and I successfully used distraction to reduce the pain of an *adult* patient. This next incident springs to mind because not only did it have the patient laughing, but also another workman close by!

My crewmate, Lisa, and I were dispatched to a thirty-odd year-old male who had been descending a work ladder while undertaking some outdoor task in the back garden of a customer's house. He'd misplaced his footing towards the last two rungs and landed very awkwardly, fracturing his ankle.

On our arrival at the patient's side, with appropriate equipment to hand, we were welcomed by a lady named Margaret, who was the owner of the house having work done to it. Also in the back garden was another man, working on some other task. On examination of the patient's ankle, it was obvious that he'd sustained a closed fracture, as it was clearly deformed and swollen. Lisa and I crouched down beside him and I began by introducing us,

"Hi. I'm Andy and this is Lisa. What's your name, buddy?"

"Gary," he replied, grimacing and obviously in a lot of pain. I then commenced some pertinent questioning regarding his symptoms, past medical history, allergies and so on. Meanwhile, Lisa began undertaking some appropriate clinical observations.

As we carried out our self-designated tasks, I offered Gary Entonox as an interim analgesic. He began self-medicating. I asked him if he would consent to me obtaining IV access and administering some Ondansetron – an anti-sickness/nausea drug – and the potent analgesic, morphine sulphate. After gaining his consent, I applied a tourniquet to his left arm and began to palpate for a suitable vein. As I was doing that, I attempted to distract him a little by asking him some open-ended questions.

"So, Gary, you're obviously working here today. What is it you've been doing?" I asked.

"Arrrgh! F**k! Yeah, I'm a plumber. I'm working on the guttering for Margaret today," he informed me as he screamed out in agony.

His profession immediately gave me an idea to try to distract him from the pain. While I continued searching for a vein, I initiated a series of profession-based wisecracks – granted, not my own original puns, but nevertheless apt. I'd attended to plumbers before, presenting in extreme agony, so I just had to remember some of the puns I'd used on those occasions. Responding to Gary's answer, I said,

"A plumber?! You'll notice that I need to *tap* on your arm to cause a vein to engorge with blood."

"Ha-ha!" he said while grinning. "Good one, mate."

"It's funny you should say that you're a plumber, because my first thought when we arrived was that you appeared a little *flush*." Lisa immediately followed with a vocalised '*boom, boom, cchhh!*', the percussive sound usually played to punctuate jokes, more uncommonly known as 'the sting'. Gary stopped grimacing and instead laughed, as too did the other workman, albeit he was merely looking on and therefore redundant. As they chuckled, I continued questioning Gary while palpating his left arm for a viable vein.

"Are you self-employed then, Gary?" I asked.

"Yeah," he replied.

"Do you two work together then?" I asked, looking at the other workman.

"No, no," said the other one, "I'm an electrician, just happen to be also working outside here today."

"Ah, right, I see. Is that your *volts-wagon* parked out the front?"

"No it's not," he replied, the intended electricians' pun going straight over his head.

"What's your name, mate? Did you witness Gary fall from the ladder, at all?"

"I'm Martin. Yeah, sort of," he replied.

"Well, I don't want to distract you. By all means, you keep *plugging* away with your work, if you wish," I said, once again with an intended pun. Martin, however, was equally oblivious to my second effort.

Gary then followed with a barrage of expletives provoked by the pain in his ankle. "Gary, Gary," I said, "there's no need for *gutter-al* language." Gary did pick up on the pun, and so Lisa immediately followed with another '*boom, boom, cchhh!*'

Lisa, recognising that humorous puns had distracted Gary from his pain, albeit momentarily, swiftly followed with, "Yeah, please *pipe down*, Gary, there's ladies present." To which I followed with a '*boom, boom, cchhh!*' Gary and Martin had a light chuckle to themselves but Gary soon felt the pain again.

After a short period of palpating, I'd located a suitable vein to cannulate, and so rummaged through the paramedic bag for the appropriate consumables. As the distractional puns had momentarily ceased, Gary began concentrating on the pain again and subsequently cried out, "Arrrgh, shit! My bloody ankle is f**kin' killin' me!" With distraction still my only analgesic option to support the Entonox at present, I had to think quickly. Martin suggested a great idea and said,

"Tell him a joke. That'll distract him."

'What a brilliant idea,' I thought. "You're a *bright spark* aren't you, Martin! You've just had a *light bulb* moment, haven't you!"

"*Boom, boom, cchhh!*" Martin responded, getting involved.

I pondered for a moment, then thought out loud, "Let me think, let me think. Um, let me think. Ah, right! Gary, here's a joke for you. A doctor heard a funny noise coming from his boiler and so called for a plumber. When the plumber arrived, he opened his tool bag and banged on the heater a couple of times with a wrench, then listened carefully for a few moments. 'It's fixed,' he said, and handed the doctor an invoice. 'Two hundred pounds, ole boy?!' the doctor replies. 'You were here ten minutes. I'm a doctor and I only make a third of that for ten minutes' work.' The plumber replies, 'Yeah, when I was a doctor, that's what I made too!'"

The joke provided some more temporary distraction for Gary, and prompted Martin to laugh as well. However, Martin then commented, "I should've been a plumber if that's true."

"Hey?" I said. "I could swap plumber for electrician in that joke and it'd still be truthful."

"Give over," Martin replied, "I don't make more than a doctor."

"Of course you do! You only have to look at a wire and the cost starts at fifty quid!" I replied. Martin went quiet and sheepishly continued with his tasks. However, the joke was having some positive effect on Gary's pain level. Then Lisa spoke.

"Gary, tell me, did you always want to be a plumber when you left school?" she asked.

"No. I always wanted to be an airline pilot," he came back with, and Lisa, possessing the gift of spontaneous wit, replied,

"Well, we all have *pipedreams*, don't we."

It may have been an old one but her pun triggered yet more laughter around the back garden, and Gary's yelling and grimacing lessened the more he laughed. It was short-lived analgesia but it was working to some degree; he appeared a lot more composed.

With a vein engorged, I donned a pair of nitrile gloves, cleaned the skin around the desired access site, and removed a cannula from its packaging. I held Gary's right arm with my left hand, and with the cannula ready in my right hand I then said,

"OK, here we go. Hopefully the blood won't *drain* from your head, Gary." Despite the circumstances, his reaction was spontaneous as he let out an immediate laugh. Martin and Lisa had a chuckle to themselves. I then hovered the cannula over my chosen venous access site. "I'll try not to hurt you, Gary... I don't want to upset you. I know you can't believe what's happened here today, but it will *sink* in." Yet more laughter resonated round the garden.

While Gary was distracted, I pierced the skin with the needle, entered the vein, and obtained and secured patent IV access. Lisa passed me the now prepared syringe of Ondansetron, which I administered first. Then she handed me the morphine sulphate. As I pushed morphine through the open port of the cannula, Lisa said,

"I hope the morphine doesn't relax you too much and cause you to take a *leak*!"

As the euphoria of the drug quickly eased Gary's pain, he said, with a smile on his face,

"You two are unbelievable, but thank you. That morphine is brilliant. Your puns are terrible but the morphine is fantastic."

We gradually watched Gary's pain visibly reduce considerably over several minutes, to the point where no more plumber or electrician puns were necessary to distract him. Job done!

A Duh Moment

I'd wondered where the history of certain jokes stemmed from and so, while writing this book, I decided to do a little research. 'An Englishman, an Irishman and a Scotsman' is the opening line of a joke trend popular in Ireland and the United Kingdom, but there are variations in how the nationalities deliver the joke. In England the punchline is usually based around the Irishman being stupid, the Scotsman being mean or miserable, and the Englishman being the clever, educated one. In Scotland and Ireland, the Englishman will typically be the stupid one. Here's a typical joke, not one of my own, granted, but here we go:

An Englishman, an Irishman and a Scotsman were sat in a pub having a pint, talking about their sons. "My son was born on St George's Day," commented the Englishman. "So, we obviously decided to call him George."

"That's a real coincidence," remarked the Scot. "My son was born on St Andrew's Day, so obviously we decided to call him Andrew."

"That's incredible, what a coincidence," said the Irishman. "Exactly the same thing happened with my son, Pancake."

Another example, though a variation on the theme, is: An Englishman walks into a bar... A Scotsman walks into a bar... A dyslexic Irishman walks into a bra...

I also specifically remember a humorous poster on the notice board in one of the many ambulance stations I worked from. It displayed the Irish fire service. On the poster was a fire engine in the background, and a car crash had evidently occurred in which the patient had been decapitated. The head was several feet away from the rest of the body. One fireman was doing chest compressions on the body, while another fireman was providing mouth to mouth ventilations to the decapitated head! This obviously absolutely pointless effort portrays the same stereotypical - and I should add, misplaced - humour that the Irish are all stupid.

Have you ever looked at something that doesn't quite make sense, where there's no logic to it whatsoever, and said out loud, 'That's Irish'? I know I have, without thinking, though I've not said it for many, many years now. Why is it, generally speaking, that the Irish get labelled as stupid? I'm very fond of the Irish. I'm very fond of the Irish accent, particularly a Dublin accent; when a lady speaks in a Dublin accent, I melt. Furthermore, I've met a lot of Irish and they're among the most intelligent people I've ever met and conversed with. Where am I going with this story? Well, I'll explain.

Siobhan and I were dispatched to an elderly gentleman complaining of abdominal pain. It wasn't a treble-nine call, only a GP's admission. The patient's GP had visited him earlier that morning and consequently arranged for him to be taken by ambulance directly to the surgical ward – as opposed to via the A&E department – for further examination.

Siobhan was a lovely Irish lady, and a rookie, trainee paramedic with only several weeks' experience.

Upon our arrival outside the patient's address, Siobhan and I made our way down the garden pathway and were immediately met by the patient stood at his open front door.

"Good morning, sir," I said. "Your carriage awaits."

"Thank you, young man. Much appreciated," he replied.

Following his grateful and well-mannered response, I then followed by introducing Siobhan and I, and also explained to him that Siobhan was a trainee. That's normal procedure in the NHS ambulance service, plus trainees are usually identified as 'Student' on their epaulettes. A patient should understand who is undertaking observations on them, whether a qualified paramedic or a trainee. With that understood, we walked along the pathway towards the ambulance, my arm linked with his arm to assist him. I then said,

"By heck, chief, you're looking very dapper. Look at your shiny shoes and suit and tie. You're only going to hospital, you know, not Buckingham Palace for an OBE!"

"I know, young man, but one likes to look jolly smart, what," he replied.

"Well, you certainly do, chief," I said. "Now, did the GP leave a letter for me to read?"

"Yes, it's in my bag, young man."

He ambled up the steps of the ambulance without needing any assistance from me at all. Once inside, I kindly asked him to position himself on the stretcher. I asked Siobhan to undertake a full set of observations while I questioned the lovely, polite man further; oh... and also while I attempted to decipher the GP's handwritten letter, which I would pass onto the ward nurse for the surgical registrar to read.

I'm sure any former or current employee of the NHS Ambulance Service knows only too well that reading a GP's handwritten letter is no easy task. You need an Enigma machine and a former employee of Bletchley Park to decipher it for you. I'm sure illegible handwriting is a pre-requisite in order to be accepted into medical school; I really do.

Anyway, while I began trying to decipher the information written by his GP, and subsequently input the patient's details onto the PRF, Siobhan continued undertaking a full set of vital observations, including a 12-lead ECG. She hadn't been on placement long but had learned how to use most of the equipment carried by ambulance personnel. Granted, she had a long learning journey ahead of her in order to be able to analyse the information. Only then would she fully understand the physiology of what's potentially occurring, allowing her to put two and two together, calculate four and treat the patient accordingly. But as I said, this particular incident was a straightforward GP admission and the patient was in good spirits. No pharmaceutical interventions were necessary, just a set of observations was all that was required.

I continued documenting the details from the GP's letter, noting the patient's name was Jack, and that he was a type 2 diabetic and, consequently, was on the prescription medication known as Metformin, amongst other medications.

A short time later, Siobhan had undertaken the observations I'd asked for, so I said, while focussing on my paperwork, "OK Siobhan, call out the observations, please." Siobhan then verbally passed me Jack's observations. They consisted of saturations of oxygen, pulse rate, blood pressure, temperature, blood glucose, pupillary response, etcetera. 'Brilliant,' I thought. "What about the ECG, Siobhan?" I asked, still looking down at my paperwork.

"I'm not sure, so I'm not, Andy. I t'ink there's something wrong with the machine," she replied. I stood up from the chair,

"Um, that's strange. It's not picking up anything, is it? Just check the leads' adhesive dots again and make sure they're sticking to the patient," I said. "Sometimes the dots lose their tackiness, or body hair can lift the dot off." So, while I was keeping an eye on the screen, Siobhan re-checked the leads.

"How's dat?" she asked as she twiddled with the leads and ensured the ECG adhesive 'dots' were sticking to the patient's limbs adequately. "Lead t'ree was a little loose."

"No, it's still not displaying a reading," I replied. "Don't worry, poor contact can cause artefact or a 'no read'. I'll check the leads."

With Jack keeping quiet and lying very still on the stretcher, I checked the upper leads that Siobhan had positioned near Jack's collar bones. They were suitably placed. I then moved towards his ankles and rolled up the hems of his trouser legs to locate where Siobhan had attached the other two leads, only to find...!

Now, it's worth me pointing out here that when undertaking an

ECG, the four leads are best placed on the arms and legs, preferably on bony prominences, not muscle. The reason being is that muscle contracts and, therefore, causes artefact or 'tremors'. Tremors cause the ECG printout or on-screen display to be illegible and it's therefore recorded on the PRF as *artefact – UTR (unable to read)*. However, what I found was hilarious, unforeseen and hadn't been mentioned to us by Jack!

He possessed two prosthetic legs! Not the advanced type designed for an amputee of today, oh no. These were like real legs with calves, shins and feet, fitted and strapped to the stumps of his thighs. Jack was wearing socks and shoes; it hadn't been at all obvious that he had prosthetic legs when we'd wandered down the pathway and into the ambulance.

Anyway, now I realised that Jack was a double lower limb amputee, I burst out laughing. Siobhan looked at me as if to say 'what's up?', so I then said,

"Come here and have a look at this." Siobhan leant over, looking at Jack's 'ankles', and said,

"What?" I then closed my hand and tapped my knuckles against each of his 'shins'.

"They're prosthetic," I announced, continuing to laugh out loud.

"What's wrong with dat?" she asked, looking confused.

"The leads need to be attached to bony prominences," I informed her. She then laughed out loud and her face turned a shade of red.

"Duh! I'm so stupid, so I am! I can't believe I've done dat!" she said, holding her palm to her forehead.

"Don't worry about it. There's nobody in the ambulance service that hasn't had a 'duh moment' at some point in their career, so welcome to the club," I said.

Siobhan went on to be a great paramedic and mentor to other students, but she did make a point of ensuring her mentees learned from her 'duh moment'.

Prank #1

I have to say first, the only reason you are about to read the following is because the 'victims' were two of my closest friends and colleagues at the time, and also because they would have done the same to me, given the chance! It just so happens that I beat them to it. Some of you may find the following story funny, absolutely hilarious, or just downright sick and twisted. As I said from the off, a dark sense of humour is common place among ambulance service personnel. Here we go.

I was working solo on a Rapid Response Vehicle (RRV) on a twelve-hour day shift. I'd been quite busy for the first several hours already. About midday, I was asked by control to park up at a stand-by location and have a well-earned breather. Unfortunately, within minutes of being parked up, I was dispatched to a thirty-odd year-old man who was having an epileptic seizure. I immediately proceeded towards the address, using blue lights and sirens and with my foot to the floor.

While driving, the dispatcher informed me that a local crew had attended the same patient several hours before, but he wasn't conveyed to hospital as it hadn't been appropriate on that occasion. They also informed me an ambulance crew were en route to back me up, but that it may be delayed due to demand at the time.

Upon arriving inside the property, I commenced the appropriate assessment and treatment, which I won't go in to, and successfully brought the patient's seizure under control. He was dazed and confused as per normal, post-epileptic seizure. Nevertheless, we had a good chat and I informed him that it was prudent that he attended hospital on this occasion, as it was his second seizure within several hours. He agreed to attend A&E without any reluctance whatsoever.

While we waited for the ambulance to arrive, we continued chatting and having a little banter. At the same time, I also began completing my documentation, during which I found the previous attending crew's completed non-conveyance form. While browsing it for particular details, I noticed that the attending crew had been Dan and John; two of my closest mates at the time, and both of the prankster type! I pondered for a moment. 'He-he-he. Great prank idea,' I thought.

A short time later, the ambulance crew arrived. I didn't know who they were, as they were out of their normal area; they'd been working away from their usual patch for some time on this particular day. Within minutes they had got the patient on board the ambulance, and off they went to hospital. Great!

When I got back into the RRV's driving seat, I decided to give my mate a call. I dialled his number and waited. 'Ring, Ring... Ring, Ring...'. When he finally answered, I kept a very low tone, an almost sombre voice. The conversation went something like this:

Dan: "Hi, Andy. How's it goin', mate?"

Me: "Hi bud. I'm OK, I suppose. Have you been busy?"

Dan: "Yeah, we've barely stopped. Have you been busy?"

Me: "Yeah, mate. I've not stopped either."

Dan: "Are you sure you're OK? You sound a bit down. A bit too quiet."

Me: "No, I'm not really. Did you attend to an epileptic seizure this morning, at all?"

Dan: "Yeah, why?" he asked with curiosity.

Me: "Well, I've just attended to him again."

Dan: "Oh, right. Is he OK, has he had another fit? Had he got worse since this morning?"

Me: "Yeah, he's changed considerably."

Dan: "In what way? Was he status epilepticus?"

Me: "He was in status when I arrived, yeah. His partner said he'd been fitting for over thirty minutes."

Dan: "Oh, right. Has he gone to A and E now then, as it's his second seizure today?"

Me: "No. He's still at home waiting to be conveyed."

Dan: "Yeah, it's busy in A and E as well as out on the road, isn't it."

Me: "No, mate, he's not waiting to be conveyed to A and E by ambulance. The police are sorting his conveyance out with the family."

Dan: "Aye! What do you mean? Oh, I see, the family are takin' him as there's no ambulances available?"

Me: "No. No. Unfortunately, he's dead."

Dan: "What?! F**k! F**k! F**k! Oh F**k! John! John! That fit we went to this morning... he's f**kin' dead! Oh shit, what'll 'appen now, Andy?"

Me: "Oh, shit. Probably a coroner's inquest. Disciplinary, dismissal. I don't entirely know, mate."

Dan: "F**k, f**k, f**k!"

Me: "Got ya! He's fine, don't panic. It was a wind-up," I managed to blurt out before practically collapsing with laughter.

Dan: "Andy, you b*****d! I f**kin' shit meself then. I'll get you back for that one, you—"

Me: "I know you will," I said, cutting him short, "I'll look forward to it. I'm gonna have to clear with control, see you later."

Dan: "OK. I'll catch-up with you later."

I hung up the line and laughed once more. After clearing with ambulance control, I was asked to go back on standby, though just a few minutes later I was dispatched to another treble-nine call. Hey-ho, there's no rest for the *WICKED*!

One Night of Passion

I don't recall being taught about the *'birds and the bees'* in primary school, nor do I recall my parents ever teaching me much about the subject, either. I do remember learning some things about human nature in the school playground at an early age.

My best recollection of sex education was when I was about thirteen years old, and I was in my secondary school biology class. The teacher was discussing sex education with the class. As the double session was nearing its end, she asked, 'Are there any questions?' She was extremely embarrassed and taken aback when a very close friend of mine raised his hand and asked, 'Do girls like anal, miss?'.

Well, the class burst out laughing. The teacher, however, shouted at him, dismissed us but kept him behind – pardon the pun! What was discussed I don't entirely know, but I do recall him telling me that she thought he was a disgusting creature and shouldn't be asking things like that at his age. She subsequently ordered him to present himself to the head teacher that same day, too!

This next story involves a middle-aged man and wife, and a teenage girl. Kevin and I were dispatched to a forty-odd year-old gentleman who was experiencing chest pain. Upon our arrival at the address given, which was on a very poverty-stricken estate, we were welcomed by a lady in her forties – the patient's wife. She kindly escorted us to the lounge where we found the patient seated on an armchair. My immediate thought was this is not time-critical. Great!

Also present in the lounge was a sort of 'rotund' teenage girl sat on the sofa a short distance away, who I took to be their daughter. I introduced Kevin and I, and then began my questioning by ascertaining his name, which I learned was Dave. I then commenced further medical questioning and assessed and treated him accordingly, using the appropriate equipment and drugs, etcetera.

Following my examination and treatment, I was satisfied that his chest pain wasn't cardiac in nature. Nevertheless, a trip to A&E was prudent and, therefore, I advised him to travel with us to hospital, to which he agreed. While still in the lounge, I kindly asked his wife and daughter whether they wished to travel with Dave in the ambulance, or make their own way to hospital. They chose to travel with Dave in the ambulance.

We were all appropriately positioned in the ambulance, Dave semi-recumbent on the stretcher, me sat to his side with my paperwork to hand, his daughter sat behind the head end of the stretcher, and his wife sat next to me. I undertook a full second set of observations and then gave Kevin the thumbs up to head for A&E.

It was during the twenty-minute journey to hospital that the humour started. Up until Kevin moved the ambulance off, nothing unusual was apparent or humorous. However, I instigated a conversation that would have me figuratively banging my head against a brick wall! All I said to Dave was,

"When we arrive at hospital, the nurse may ask your wife and daughter to wait in the—"

"It's not my daughter," he said, interrupting me. On that, I glanced at the young girl and the lady sat beside me.

"I thought it was your wife and daughter, I do apologise to all three of you," I said.

"That is my wife," he said, pointing to the lady sat next to me. "But she is my girlfriend," he said, referring to the teen. "She's carrying my baby." I was taken aback a little, because the wife and teenager seemed comfortable in each other's company. After a short pause, I then said to the young girl,

"Oh, right. How old are you, love?"

"Seventeen," she said.

"Seventeen, hey. How many weeks pregnant are you, then?" I asked out of curiosity; pregnancy wasn't blatantly obvious as she was already on the *bonnie* side anyway.

"Twelve weeks," she replied.

'You're a girl of very few words,' I thought to myself, but instead said, "Well, congratulations to you... um... to you both, I suppose. How do you feel about this situation?" I asked Dave's wife.

"It is what it is," she aloofly replied.

Well, I was intrigued by this point, so I just had to pry further; I just felt like being a nosey-sod, to be honest. So, looking back at Dave, I said,

"So, that's your wife... but that's your girlfriend who's carrying your unborn. How did this all happen?"

"Well my wife, Sharon, already knew my girlfriend, Lyndsey, from work. My wife told me that Lyndsey needed some painting doing around her flat, so Sharon asked if I'd do it. I'm a good painter, so I said yes," he explained.

'And? Did she trip over a tin of Dulux and get pregnant?!' I thought. I continued looking at him, and he looked back at me as if to say, 'What? You need more of an explanation?'

"Go on," I said, "I'm intrigued."

"Well, while I was working there we had a good laugh, got on really well, and one thing led to another. If you know what I mean?"

"Right. Blimey. How long ago was that then?" I asked, ignoring my paperwork due to being preoccupied with the romantic *'love story'*.

"Three weeks ago," he promptly replied.

I couldn't believe what I'd heard! My mind spun. 'Nobody his age could possibly be that naive and stupid!' I thought, but instead said,

"Sorry? Sorry, Dave? Lyndsey is twelve weeks pregnant, you met each other three weeks ago, and you think she's carrying your unborn baby?"

I know it sounds rude of me while all three were present, but I do have a reputation for not beating about the bush, both back then, when this incident occurred, to the present day!

"Lyndsey said it is," he replied.

"It is his," Lyndsey stated, quickly following up on Dave's comment. I turned my head to his wife, Sharon.

"What do you think? Am I hearing right, here?" I asked her.

"I said it can't be his, but she insists it is, and he believes it's his," Sharon replied. Part of me thought, 'Thank you! Somebody's on my wavelength!' Another part of me thought, 'Oh my god, even Sharon isn't the fizziest drink in the fridge'. I turned to Dave once again and said,

"Dave. Think about it, pal. Lyndsey is twelve weeks pregnant and you only met her three weeks ago. Yeah?"

"Yeah. Three weeks tomorrow, actually," he confirmed.

"Dave, do the mathematics, mate," I said.

"What do you mean?" he asked.

Now, picture me looking at each of them in turn, observing for at least one of them to understand my problem with the mathematical biology of it. Not one of them could understand or grasp my point, so I thought I'd question Lyndsey a bit more... pointedly.

"Lyndsey. How's it possible for Dave to be the father of your unborn?" I asked quite sternly.

"It's his. I haven't been with anyone else," she said. I looked at her with a *'come on, really?'* sort of expression. She just looked away from me as if she knew exactly what she was up to and what I was getting at. Some poor, middle-aged man was going to cop for somebody else's responsibility. I almost felt sorry for Dave. His naivety might not only cost him a future fortune, but also end his marriage. I wanted the penny to drop so he didn't destroy his life through somebody else's deceit.

We were approaching the hospital, so I thought 'sod it, I'll see if Kevin can help me out'. As we rolled under the A&E department's ambulance parking canopy, Kevin vacated his seat and opened the back doors.

"Everything all right?" Kevin asked. I looked at him and shook my head in despair. Kevin furrowed his eyebrows and said, "What's wrong?"

"I'll tell you in a minute, Kev," I said.

We wheeled Dave into A&E and along the corridor, directing Sharon and Lyndsey to the waiting area. Due to how busy it was, we were asked to wait in the corridor until a cubicle became available. While Kevin and I were waiting, and with Dave still positioned on the stretcher, I said,

"Kev, help me out here, mate. The young girl, Lyndsey, is twelve weeks pregnant. She isn't Dave's daughter, she's his girlfriend. She insists that Dave is the father of her baby, but they only met three weeks ago, in fact three weeks tomorrow. I've tried tellin' him that the baby can't be his. He said that she said it is, so it must be," I explained. Kevin frowned, looked at Dave and said,

"Andy's right. You don't have to be Carol Vorderman to figure that one out."

"Well, she said the baby's mine, so I believe her," he replied. Kev and I just looked at each other, laughed and shook our heads in despair. 'Forget it,' I thought, 'there's no point. He won't listen.'

We handed Dave over to the triage nurse, replaced the bed linen and vacated the hospital. While driving back to the station, Kevin and I couldn't help but laugh while discussing the incident and the fact that three adults – well, two adults and a teenager who would be classed as an adult on her next birthday – were all too stupid to realise how impossible it was for Dave to be the unborn baby's biological father. Unbelievable! Mind you, I strongly felt that Lyndsey knew exactly what she was doing, and Sharon seemed to get it. So perhaps there was another explanation.

In hindsight, it may well be that Dave was actually more than happy to replace his wife with a seventeen-year-old, and the baby was the happy excuse! And perhaps his wife was more than happy to be shot of him! As for Lyndsey, the pregnant teenager, she probably saw Dave as a better bet for her future than whoever did the deed.

I'll conclude the above story with that old saying: one night of passion can lead to a life of misery!

Time-Critical!

This next incident once again involved Izzie and myself. We were on a nightshift and had been very busy from the start of the shift, right up to the time a further call was passed to us. It was approximately 1am and we were dispatched to attend to a seventy-odd year-old gentleman who had collapsed. The caller, the patient's wife, had told control that her husband was unconscious.

On our arrival we were presented with a huge Victorian house, with ample front garden and a long pathway that led from the roadside to the front door. I brought the vehicle to a halt. Izzie quickly vacated her seat and grabbed the paramedic bag from the saloon, then began to make her way down the long garden pathway. I followed closely behind.

It was absolutely pitch black: I couldn't see my hands in front of my face, and there was no garden or pathway lighting whatsoever. Izzie, slightly ahead of me, flicked her jacket-torch on, as did I, but the visibility was still poor to say the least, the very least. As we carefully made our way towards the front door, I could see the hallway lit and the door ajar, and also heard dogs barking. 'I hope they're locked away,' I thought. 'They sound huge.' Then Izzie called out,

"Shit!"

"What's up?" I asked.

"I've just slipped on moss, for f**k's sake. Where's the garden lights?!"

We carried on along the pathway, then I slipped but managed to remain on my feet. "Shit!" I said. "Keep going, Izzie, be careful though, this pathway is covered in moss. We're nearly at the front door."

When we reached the door, we wandered inside. The inside of the house was beautifully decorated. There were huge mirrors, amazing paintings hung on the walls, and the flooring was covered with beige coloured, obviously very expensive carpet. The house must have been worth over half a million at least, a good amount back then.

"Hello! Paramedics! Hello!" I shouted.

"Up here!" a lady's voice called.

Izzie and I walked up the first carpeted, spiral staircase, along a landing and then up another staircase, along another landing and then into a bedroom. There we found the lady – the caller. Her husband, our patient, was laid on the floor, not moving. We quickly began assessing him, and it became clear that he had a patent airway and was breathing for himself, adequately too. Nonetheless, he was unconscious. This was potentially very, very serious.

"What's your husband's name?" I asked the patient's wife.

"Arthur," she answered.

"And your name is?"

"Margaret," she replied as she looked on, appearing obviously concerned about Arthur's health status. "He's not going to die, is he?" Margaret asked. I wasn't going to answer that question, instead I continued to reassure her while Izzie and I continued our assessment.

During our assessment, Izzie began sniffing, and then quietly said, "Andy, I think he's been incontinent. I can smell poo."

"Yeah, I think you're right. I can, too," I replied.

A short time passed and a full set of observations were complete. I looked at Izzie and said, "Right, his obs are within normal parameters, but I think he's had some sort of syncopal episode and been incontinent. Nevertheless, he'll have to go in as an unconscious collapse, query cause." I glanced towards the door. "I don't fancy carrying him down the stairs on our own though, not while he's unconscious. We'll treat it as a time-critical incident, and ask for another crew to attend. I'll have a little chat with Margaret. Can you contact control for back-up, hot response, no divert, please Izzie?"

I stood and turned to Margaret and said, "Right, Margaret. Arthur's observations and ECG are within normal parameters but there's a reason why he's remaining unconscious; not asleep, unconscious. So, we'll have to take him into hospital. OK? Don't worry though," I explained. "Can you gather some essential overnight things together for him, please?"

Margaret left the bedroom to do as I'd asked. Meanwhile, Izzie undertook a second set of observations on Arthur, while I began to make my way from the bedroom to the ambulance to fetch the carry-chair, ready for when the back-up crew arrived. As I walked along the landing towards the second staircase, then along the first landing towards the spiral staircase, I noticed footprints along the carpet. It looked faintly like dog poo. 'Oh shit!' I thought.

When I reached the front door, I carefully ambled back along the garden pathway towards the ambulance. I fetched the carry-chair and blankets and proceeded back down the path, carefully! As I entered the hallway once again and began walking up the stairs, I looked over my shoulder, only to see the footprints of my size nine boots blatantly leaving dog poo on the carpet with each step that I took. 'Oh shit!' I thought once again.

I checked the bottom of the sole of my left boot. Nothing. I checked my right boot and it was covered in doggy doo-doo. 'Oh, no,' I thought. Regardless, I carried on ascending the stairs and back to the bedroom.

"Izzie," I said, "I don't think Arthur has been incontinent. I've stood in dog poo on the pathway, it's all over the carpet! Let me check your boots." While Izzie was still knelt next to Arthur, who remained unconscious, I checked her boots and there was doggy doo-doo on one of her boots, too.

"You've got dog shit on your boots," I said. "Anyway, how is he?"

"Oh, I hate dog poo," she said. "His obs are still within normal parameters. The crew should be here soon, hopefully."

A short time later, Margaret entered the bedroom with a look of horror on her face. "Right, Margaret," I said, "we've got another crew on the way, due to the—"

"Can you both take your shoes off, please?" she asked, interrupting me. Izzie and I looked at each other, confused.

"I'm sorry?" I said.

"There's dog mess on my carpet. Can you take your shoes off, please?"

I couldn't believe what I was hearing, and so stood up from my knelt position and said to Margaret, "I'm sorry about your carpet, Margaret, but we can't remove our shoes, we'll be leaving with your unconscious husband soon. There's obviously some dog sh... mess outside, but we couldn't see where we were walking as there's no garden lights."

"Yes, I appreciate that. I've not had chance to clean the pathway of the dogs' mess yet, but my carpet is covered. Can you kindly remove your shoes until you get to the bottom of the stairs, please?" she asked.

"Margaret... Arthur is unconscious and we don't know why. There's another crew on the way to help us lift him down the two staircases, one of which is spiral. I do apologise for the mess but we're not going to delay conveying your husband to definitive care for the sake of your carpet. If you'd cleaned the bloody pathway during daylight, then we wouldn't be having this discussion, would we?" I said, quite sternly.

"I shall be making a complaint to the ambulance service," she said, and then she stormed out of the bedroom. A short time later, my hand portable radio alarmed.

"Go ahead, over," I said.

"Roger. Andy, we're here. Where are you?" Steve asked.

"Follow the dog shit footprints, mate! Oh, and check your boots before you come up," I replied. Izzie began laughing and said,

"These lines are recorded, you know."

"I don't care," I said. Then my radio sounded again.

"Go ahead, over."

"Andy, I've got dog poo on my boot," Steve said. Me and Izzie burst out laughing. Composing myself just enough, I replied to Steve with,

"Roger. Join the club. Just get up here, regardless. We've got a time-critical patient here."

A minute or so passed, but Steve and his crewmate hadn't arrived at the bedroom.

"Where are they?" I asked Izzie. A minute or two later, Steve and his crewmate turned up. "Right, guys—"

"That woman's just stopped us along the landing and asked us to take our shoes off," Steve said, interrupting me.

"Oh, for f**k's sake! What did you say to her?"

"I said no we bloody well won't, and then we carried on along the landing... f**k's her problem?" he replied. I just laughed and said,

"She's not cleaned up the pathway after their dogs, and there's no garden lighting, so don't worry about it. She's more concerned about her carpet than she is her husband, by the looks of it!"

Between the four of us, we lifted and positioned Arthur onto the carry-chair, wheeled him out of the bedroom, along the landing, down the stairs, along the other landing and down the spiral staircase to the front door, leaving behind us further trails of dog poo footprints on the carpet. We lifted the carry-chair over the threshold and along the garden pathway to the ambulance, treading doggy doo-doo onto the floor of the saloon.

As we carefully lifted, positioned and strapped Arthur securely on the stretcher, Margaret suddenly appeared at the open back door of the ambulance.

"I'll be putting a complaint in about the state of my carpets, you know! And a claim for compensation, too," she said. I then turned to face her and replied with,

"Listen, Margaret. Your husband is potentially in grave danger. Furthermore, two ambulance crews are going to be off the road after we've handed Arthur over to the A and E doctors, because we now have to clean our boots before we go into somebody else's house, and also to thoroughly clean the ambulances. All because you've not bothered to: one, fit garden lights, and two, because you 'aven't cleaned the ample amounts of dog shit from your pathway. So, by all means, put a complaint in," I said sternly.

Margaret didn't reply, she just stormed off down the pathway and back into her stunning abode. Granted, the carpet was covered in dog faeces, but that was mainly her fault. I never did receive a complaint, nor did I ever find out why Arthur remained unconscious throughout the whole incident.

A Duty of Care

As you may well be aware, particularly from the number of television documentaries about the ambulance service and A&E hospitals aired these days, ambulance service personnel attend to a lot of alcohol-fuelled incidents. They usually consist of collapses, fights, assault, affray, etcetera. This next incident involved an assault on a young adult, but with a slight twist in the conclusion.

Jay, a technician, and I were on a Saturday nightshift, and were wandering around the streets in the ambulance, waiting for a call to come in after 'kick-out' time, so to speak. At approximately midnight, we were called to a public house to attend to a young lad who'd been assaulted outside; a typical weekend call for ambulance and police personnel. The bouncers had brought the situation under control but deemed it necessary to call treble-nine as the lad had a bruised eye.

When we rolled up on scene, the lad was extremely keen to board the ambulance, before I even had chance to get out of the cab! He practically ran to the vehicle and stood next to the side door; I was surprised he didn't help himself and just open the door and clamber aboard!

I vacated the cab, entered the saloon and welcomed the young lad inside. He sat down and I ascertained his name and began questioning him as to what had happened.

"I came out of the pub, right. This lad started on me for no reason and just punched me in the face," he explained. Jay commenced some basic observations while I continued questioning.

"So, were you knocked out, at all?" I asked, while carefully observing his mannerisms, pupil size, and the eye he'd been punched in.

"No, was I f**k. His punch was shit, f**kin' weak, man. I'll knock him out next time I see him!" he exclaimed. Ambulance personnel – and I assume the police, too – would be very, very rich people if we received a pound for every time we'd heard that from a drunken teenager: 'I'll knock him out the next time I see him!' Trust me, it's a common statement, post assault. Anyway, I continued.

"Ah, really? Why didn't you knock him out while you had the chance to?" I asked, being sarcastic.

"He ran off, 'cause he was scared of me," he stated. Jay, still undertaking some obs, smirked at me.

As several minutes passed, I was content that his slightly bruised eye didn't need any hospital attention, therefore, I passed my professional opinion to the teen.

"OK. You don't need hospital, so we'll just complete some paperwork and you can be on your way, buddy," I said.

"No, I want to go to A and E," he stated.

"You don't need to, mate. You'll be fine. Just get yourself off home," I kindly suggested. He started shuffling about a bit, which stirred a sixth sense in me.

"No, I really want to go to hospital. I'd rather go with you guys 'cause you know what you're doing if I get worse or anythin'." My suspicions heightened. I was used to this spiel.

"Where do you live?" I asked.

"About five minutes from Saint Richard's," he informed me.

"Ah, right," I replied. Jay looked at me as if to say, 'I know what you're thinking, Andy.' I pondered for a moment before saying, "Listen, pal. You really don't need A and E. Plus, it's really busy tonight. You'll be waiting for hours," I emphasised. He just continued fidgeting with his mobile phone, and intermittently looking at me, then back to his mobile phone.

"Are we going to A and E or what?" he asked with a little attitude.

"Are you sure you want to?" I asked. "A and E's are really busy tonight." Jay was once again picking up on the point of my questioning.

"Maybe, mate, but I'll be in and out. I guarantee it. I won't be in long at all," he emphasised.

"How do you know?" I asked. "It's very busy and you won't be a priority patient, I can tell you that right now," I said. He looked at me with a smug grin, and gave me a cocky wink.

"Trust me, with this minor injury I'll be in and out of that door in no time at all," he said with sheer confidence in his tone.

"You only have a slight red mark on your left eye where he punched you. A and E will do nothing for you," I explained, hoping that I could persuade him to accept my professional medical opinion, and so we could soon become clear and available for somebody who might *really* need an ambulance.

"I wanna go to A and E, and I pay your f**kin' wages, so take me!" he said aggressively, probably thanks to the bit of Dutch courage he'd gained from the alcohol.

"You pay my wages?" I asked. "How's that? What do you work as?"

"Hey?"

"I said, what do you work as if you pay my wages?" He paused and looked a little stumped.

"Well, I don't work, but my mum and dad do, so they pay your wages," he said. Jay and I looked at each other and grinned. We'd heard the same comment from drunken revellers so many times during our careers. It never loses its humour.

"OK. We'll pop you through to A and E, then," I said. I then looked at Jay and gave him a very subtle nod of my head. He reciprocated a nod of his head, and then vacated the saloon and positioned himself in the driver's seat. "When you're ready, mate!" I shouted.

"OK, Andy. Moving off!" Jay replied.

As we ambled along, with Jay negotiating bends, traffic lights and roundabouts, I began completing my PRF. Meanwhile, the patient was fixated on his mobile phone, only occasionally glancing away from his device to answer my questions.

After approximately twenty minutes, we arrived at A&E. Jay brought the vehicle to a standstill, vacated his seat and opened the side door.

"Come on, pal, we're here," I said. The lad put his phone in his pocket, stepped off the ambulance and took an extremely rapid, multi-directional look around the grounds.

"Where the f**k are we?!" he asked.

"We're at Saint Luke's A and E," I stated.

"Saint f**kin' Luke's?!" he repeated, with aggression in his voice. "I live five f**kin' minutes from Saint Richard's, for f**k's sake!" he exclaimed.

"Ah, but we have a duty of care and we are obliged to take you to the nearest A and E department that can provide definitive care; not the hospital that's closest to your home," I informed him.

"Oh, for f**k's sake," he said. "How the f**k am I gonna get home from here?"

"Taxi?" I replied. "It won't be a big yellow one with fluorescent stripes though, more like a lovely, clean and shiny black Mondeo."

"I can't afford a f**kin' taxi! Why didn't you just take me to Saint

Richard's?" he asked. I looked at Jay, then looked at him and said,

"I've already told you. We're obliged to take you to the nearest A and E. Saint Richard's is approximately one mile further from the pub we picked you up at than Saint Luke's is. So, as we have a duty of care, we brought you here."

"Shit, man," he said, with his palm over his forehead.

"Don't worry, you'll be in and out in no time at all. You guaranteed it. I trust you!" I turned to Jay but then back to the lad, as if I'd just remembered something. "Oh, and by the way. This is an emergency ambulance, not a taxi service! Use it, don't abuse it!" I said with a huge, smug grin on my face.

Cunning Tactics

It was a lovely summer's evening and Jed, an ambulance technician, and I were sat in the station mess room. At approximately 8pm, a treble-nine call was passed to us via my radio. We were dispatched to attend to a nineteen year-old male who was acting in a strange manner. He and his friends were reportedly gathered along a bridle path, drinking alcohol, and they'd become concerned about their friend's unusual behaviour.

Jed and I proceeded to the location, but we had to park the ambulance on the roadside and walk, with equipment in hand, along the pathway to reach the group and our patient. After a short walk, we located the five of them. They'd evidently been drinking, as there were empty cans and bottles scattered around them. Jed immediately began questioning the group about the history of events leading up to their friend's odd behaviour, while I began assessing the teenaged patient.

"Evening, guys and gals. What's going on then?" Jed asked.

"We're not sure. He just started acting really weird, like in a way we've never seen him act before," a young girl explained.

"Have you all been drinking?" Jed asked.

"Yeah," the same girl replied.

With the other members of the group remaining mute, Jed kindly asked them to clear up all their cans, bottles and other litter, and put it into their carrier bags. "There's no need to litter this pathway, you know, folks. It's disrespectful, disgraceful, and illegal. D'ya know that?" he asked them, steadily making eye contact with the whole group.

Meanwhile, I continued conversing with the young man, having established that his name was Paul. The smell of alcohol was evident on his breath, but I smelt a rat, too! There was more to his mannerisms and odd behaviour than just alcohol intoxication.

"How much have you had to drink, Paul?" I asked, while I undertook further vital observations.

"Four cans of Foster's. That's all," he answered, staring at the sky, moving his head side to side, and stroking his right arm repeatedly.

"Really? Only four cans of Foster's? You've had some drugs, haven't you? Come on, be honest," I said.

"No, no mate. I 'aven't had any, man," he answered, shaking his head and also focussing on the palms of his hands as if there was something walking on them.

Overall, I was satisfied with Paul's initial observations, including his blood sugar levels. But my sixth sense had heightened even further, so I refrained from obtaining all of his vitals; save for one particular test to extract some truth from him!

I approached Jed, who was still questioning the group of teens about what they'd drank that evening and whether they had taken any recreational drugs. Interrupting him, I took him to one side.

"He's not tellin' me the truth, so I'm gonna get it from him using a cunning tactic. Just go with it, OK?" I said.

"Why, what are you going to do?" he asked with intrigue. I didn't answer, I just gave him a wink of the eye, and then walked back over to Paul.

"Right, Paul. I'm gonna give you another chance to come clean with me and tell me exactly how much you've drank tonight, and also what drugs you've taken. OK?"

"I've only had four cans. I promise," he stated.

Now, from my experience, the number of cans a teen admits to drinking can usually be doubled, and then add some spirits to the formula. I couldn't see anything on the pathway other than beer bottles and cans, but I wasn't convinced. I continued probing a little further, but Paul insisted that he'd only had four cans of Foster's and hadn't used any drugs that day or evening.

While I continued attempting to get the truth from Paul, I heard Jed trying to obtain the truth from the rest of the group, but they also denied the use of any drugs.

We'd been on scene for fifteen minutes or so and were being lied to by the whole group. Unfortunately, ambulance personnel don't carry truth serum or a polygraph machine, so I decided to use another tactic, taking advantage of Paul's lack of medical knowledge and being unaware of the medical purpose of a particular piece of equipment. I removed the SpO2 monitor from the paramedic bag and prepared to place it onto Paul's index finger.

To keep it simple, the SpO2 device is used to measure the percentage of oxygenated blood in the body, and also to give an estimated pulse rate. However, Paul didn't know that!

"OK, Paul. I'm gonna place this probe on your index finger and step a few feet away from you. I want you to shout the figure out that appears on the LED display. OK?" I explained.

"What does this do?" he asked.

"Ah, well, I'll tell you in a minute," I said. "Just shout the figure out for me, please."

I walked away, just to add effect to the illusion. Paul stood to his feet, swaying side to side while doing so. Jed and the group of teens looked on with interest. I stood there and studied Paul while he stared at the LED display of the SpO2 monitor, and then I said,

"Does the display have a figure of ninety-five percent or above on it, Paul?" I asked. I turned to look at Jed, who had a huge grin on his face, evidently trying not to laugh out loud, and gave him a subtle wink.

"Yeah, it does," Paul replied. He continued to sway from side to side, so I walked back over to him and asked him to sit down on the tarmacked path.

"Let's have a look at the figure," I said. Glancing at the monitor, I could see that his SpO2 measurement displayed ninety-seven percent. That was no surprise to me, I knew it would be above ninety-five percent, but Paul wasn't to know what that percentage meant.

"What does it mean?" he asked.

"What it means, Paul, is that you're lying to me. A figure over ninety-five percent means you have smoked cannabis. It's a very expensive and very accurate machine," I explained. "So, tell me the truth. Have you had some cannabis tonight?" At last he answered my question, and without any hesitation whatsoever.

"Yeah, mate. I'm sorry for lying to you," he said with some remorse.

I still wasn't satisfied, so I extended the tactic further. "Have you had anything *other than* cannabis and four cans of lager, Paul?" I asked, expecting more lies to come my way.

"No, that's it. I promise," he replied. I looked at the SpO2 monitor and it still displayed ninety-seven percent. I unwrapped and removed a nasal oxygen tube from its packaging, attached it to an O2 cylinder, and placed the nasal probes appropriately into Paul's nostrils. I then turned the oxygen on and set the dosage to one-litre per minute. I turned to Paul and said,

"Now, Paul. If that percentage increases to ninety-eight or above, then I know you've had other drugs. Ninety-nine would suggest cocaine. Do you understand?" I knew it would increase because I had administered a very small amount of oxygen. Moments later, Paul stared at the display and then exhaled a long sigh. "What does it say, Paul?" I asked.

"It's flickering from ninety-eight, ninety-nine percent," he replied, with a tone of resignation in his voice. I shook my head at him in disappointment.

"Well, have you? Have you had some cocaine tonight?" I asked. He placed his face into the palms of his hands and replied,

"Yeah, I've snorted cocaine, too. I'm sorry for lying." I immediately switched off the oxygen cylinder and removed the nasal tubing from his nose.

"Why didn't you just tell me?" I asked. He looked at me with guilt and remorse.

"Because I don't wanna get in trouble with the police, or you," he said. I looked at him with a friendly, reassuring expression.

"I'm not a copper, and you're not going to get in trouble with the police. I'm not going to report you. I am going to advise that you come to A and E with us though, for observations at least. You're gathered along a bridle path and acting strange, according to your friends that is. You've had cannabis, cocaine, and I think you've had more drink than you've admitted to," I said.

"I've only had four cans of Foster's, but I've also drank spirits. That's why I feel so sick," he explained.

"What spirits have you had?" I asked.

"Dunno," he replied. I shook my head at him once more and then left him sat on the tarmac and approached Jed, who grinned at me and then started laughing. The other members of the group were none the wiser of our reasons for laughing, so Jed, in an over-exaggerated tone, said,

"Right, let's do the same test on this lot, Andy!"

The group all began talking over one another, reluctant to take the test, and then all, without hesitation, confessed to smoking cannabis and snorting cocaine. Jed and I held back further laughter and did our utmost best to look deadly serious. While Jed lectured the group about the dangers involved in taking drugs, we heard Paul vomiting, so I walked the several feet back over to him. I studied the unpleasant mess on the ground... It was bright green.

"You've had absinthe haven't you, Paul?" I asked. After composing himself post-puke, he was able to stand and reply.

"I don't know what it was, mate, but I feel better for hurling."

A short time later, we all began walking back towards the ambulance, ensuring that Paul, who was in the worst state of all of them, was steady enough on his feet. We had to occasionally support him to keep him from falling, and upon arriving back at the roadside, Paul staggered aboard the vehicle and laid himself on the stretcher. One of the girls kindly volunteered to travel with him, while the others chose to walk home.

When we arrived at A&E, Jed went to book Paul in at reception, while I gave my handover to the triage nurse. I explained to her the history of events, what Paul's vital observations were, and also how I managed to extract the truth from him. The nurse laughed, shook her head, and called me a cunning, cheeky little monkey!

Congested

I was often asked whether I ever abused the privilege of being permitted to drive an ambulance or an RRV using blue lights and sirens; that is, when it wasn't a treble-nine call and I just wanted to get where I wanted to go, quicker. The answer is absolutely not! The consequences for any emergency service personnel abusing such a privilege would more than likely be dismissal; much worse if involved in a road traffic collision, either with a vehicle or a pedestrian. With this in mind, this next story had me and my good friend and colleague, Dale, in absolute stitches.

We were on a twelve-hour day shift one lovely summer's day. We'd vacated the A&E department after handing over a patient to the triage nurse, and were heading back to the station for a brew. It was about midday and the traffic was horrendous for some reason; we didn't know why at the time, but it would eventually become apparent. It meant that the route back to station was congested, bumper to bumper.

While sat in the traffic, Dale said, "What are you doing for lunch?"

"I was thinking of stopping at the Express or petrol station for a sandwich," I replied.

Remaining very bored and hot, a further ten minutes passed and we'd moved about five metres further along the road. Then, to our relief, the dispatcher contacted us.

"Five-five. Go ahead, over," I said.

"Roger, five-five. I'm passing a RED call to your monitor now, over." The address was passed to us via the monitor, and Dale switched the blue lights and sirens on and attempted to make progress, albeit very slowly. The traffic ahead had barely anywhere to go in order to allow us to advance.

It was absolutely chock-a-block! Nevertheless, the road users did

93

their utmost best to allow us slow, steady movement. Dale carefully negotiated his way through the traffic, weaving in and out from left lane to right lane and vice-versa. Cars parted to the left and right, like Moses parting the seas. It took Dale ten minutes to do approximately one mile through the traffic jam. Typically, some drivers panic when an emergency service vehicle is behind them, and so there were countless car horns beeping as people became irate at other drivers' silly manoeuvres.

After approximately fifteen minutes of driving, barely reaching any speed above fifteen miles per hour, we reached the culprit of the congestion... gas works and temporary traffic signals. However, just as we reached that point, we were stood down from the treble-nine call as a nearer ambulance had become clear and available to respond instead. Consequently, Dale switched off the blue lights and sirens and waited for the temporary traffic light signals to change to green.

It just so happened that the next left turn was the entrance to the supermarket, so I contacted ambulance control.

"Go ahead five-five," the controller said.

"Roger. Is it OK if we pop into the supermarket to pick up some lunch? We're obviously still contactable if a job comes in, over," I replied.

With permission granted, Dale indicated left, entered the supermarket grounds and parked up. "Can you imagine what people are gonna think now?" said Dale with a laugh. "They don't know we've been stood down from an emergency. They're gonna think we've blue-lighted through traffic to get to the supermarket."

"I know," I replied, also with a laugh, "it looks terrible to all those stuck in that traffic."

As we vacated the cab, a man came hurtling towards us with anger on his face. At first I thought, 'he's not coming over to speak to *us*'.

I was wrong!

"Oi! You two!" he shouted. In spite of what we'd just been saying, Dale and I were taken aback a little. We looked at each other as if to say 'f**k's his problem?!' We stood still, waiting for the man to get closer.

"Is there a problem?" I asked. By now he was within a few feet of us and still looked very angry, displaying an aggressive facial expression.

"Yeah, there f**kin' is!" he shouted.

"Really? Enlighten me," I said, calmly.

"You have just used your blue lights and sirens to get through that traffic jam so you can get to the shop!" Dale and I looked at each other and laughed.

"I'm afraid you're mistaken. We were en route to an emergency, but we were stood down as a nearer ambulance became clear to respond," I explained.

"B*****ks!" he shouted. "I'll be putting a f**kin' complaint in. I'll have your f**kin' jobs, I tell you!" he said with hostility and a bucket load of aggressive body language.

"That's fine. Can you write down the phone number, please?" I asked Dale. "That'll connect you directly to the station manager," I said to the man. Dale sat in the cab and jotted down the phone number onto a piece of scrap paper. He then approached the irate man to hand the paper to him. As he did, the man aggressively stepped forward. For a moment I poised myself, ready to defend Dale if absolutely necessary.

"Kiss goodbye to your jobs, lads," he said.

"You're mistaken. I guarantee our jobs are safe. Your behaviour is unnecessary," I said.

"You f**kin' d**kheads!" he shouted. "I'm a police officer, and what you've done is illegal," he stated.

I couldn't believe the unfounded accusation the off-duty police officer was making, and so refused to leave it there. Facing him, I said,

"Ah, a copper? Have you pulled in to pick up some coffee and doughnuts for your next stakeout?" I asked in a humorous, sarcastic manner.

"Don't be funny, you f**kin' d**khead. This is serious," he said.

By now, Dale and I were laughing at the off-duty copper's hostile approach to what was an innocent, coincidental misunderstanding on his part.

"Yeah, it is serious. If you're a copper, then you should know better. Are you telling me that you've never been stood down from an emergency call because a nearer unit became available?" I asked. He paused for a moment.

"Yeah, but if I'm in heavily congested traffic, I keep the blue lights on until I reach a quieter road," he said, as the now heated debate was beginning to attract the attention of some supermarket customers. But I refused to let the allegation go.

"Ah, right. So you drive illegally on blue lights then, *after* you've been stood down? You bloody hypocrite," I said. "What's your collar number? I don't like your attitude, it's disgraceful. And you're also abusing your authoritative position. Can you see anybody else pulling in to make false allegations?" I asked, while broadly smiling.

As we continued exchanging comments, two men wandered over to us.

"Is everything OK, guys? Do you need any help?" one of the men asked. Before I had chance to reply, the copper piped up,

"I'm an off-duty police officer. Just be—"

"I don't give a flying f**k what you are, you're hassling these two paramedics. What have they done, hey?" he said, interrupting the copper. Dale and I couldn't help but laugh in response to the man's well-intentioned intervention.

"They've used their blue lights to get through a traffic jam so they can come here to the supermarket," he alleged. The Good Samaritan laughed and then said,

"Do you have proof? Were you sat in the ambulance with them, were you? Or are you just assuming that they used blue lights to get to the supermarket? Could it be that they were stood down because a nearer vehicle became clear and available?" he asked.

I thought, 'This guy seems to be knowledgeable about ambulance service emergency call occurrences,' but I chose not to say anything to him.

"I doubt it. I'll be ringing the station as soon as I get home," the copper said. "Kiss goodbye to your jobs, lads."

"Kiss my arse," I replied. He then stormed off towards his car. Dale and I looked at each other and burst out laughing. I was angry at the accusations he'd made, but we laughed knowing how mistaken the police officer was and how he'd soon find out.

Liaising with the Good Samaritan, it became apparent that he was actually an off-duty paramedic from another county, visiting family in the area, which is why he'd said what he had.

While walking around the supermarket, Dale and I continued to chuckle intermittently. We also had a bet between us, which was: will the copper *really* contact the station manager and complain, or not? I bet Dale that he would. Dale bet me that he wouldn't.

What I hadn't realised was that while Dale was sat in the cab, jotting down the ambulance station's phone number, he had also started the voice recorder on his mobile phone, and so the majority of the heated exchange was stored for future use, if necessary.

Several hours went by, and Dale and I had attended to several more treble-nine calls. After clearing from A&E, control asked us to return to the ambulance station. Upon arriving inside the station, we were immediately told by the station manager that he wanted to see us in his office within five minutes.

"I win," I said to Dale with a smile on my face, as I approached the kitchen to make a brew for us both.

"Shit. We're in for a b*****kin'," he said.

"Give over. We've done nothing wrong, don't worry. He'll just be checking up that we didn't abuse our blue light privileges, that's all," I reassured Dale. A few minutes later, we proceeded to the manager's office. I couldn't help but laugh out loud while walking down the corridor, ready to hear what truth or lies had been said by the officer.

We entered the manager's office and both sat down. Dale looked quite concerned. I, however, had a big grin on my face. The manager explained to us that he'd received a complaint regarding the misuse of blue lights and sirens. He said that the complainant – an off-duty police officer – stated that we were stuck in heavily congested traffic, when all of a sudden we were nudging our way through traffic using blue lights and sirens, causing absolute havoc on the road. Then, upon reaching the temporary traffic signals, the blue lights were switched off and we entered the supermarket car park.

While the manager was telling us this, I was grinning and repeatedly nodded my head as he spoke. At the end of recounting the officer's allegation, he paused for a moment and then asked,

"Is the allegation true?" Dale and I looked at each other and burst out laughing. The manager didn't see the funny side... until I explained.

"It's true," I said, "all true. However, there's a twist to his version of the truth. If you ask control, they'll confirm that we were passed a treble-nine call while stuck in solid traffic, due to the gas works going on." I then explained how Dale had slowly negotiated his way through the jam, but as we arrived at the traffic signals, we were stood down. "It seemed like a good time to nip into the supermarket to pick up some lunch, so we asked control for permission."

Dale then played the voice recording on his mobile phone. After the manager had listened to the recording, he contacted ambulance control. They confirmed the timeline of events and, therefore, confirmed our innocence. I did receive a 'slapped wrist' for my sarcasm and occasional swearing during the altercation with the copper, but the manager was happy with our version of events and the corroboration from the dispatcher. In the end he saw the funny side, too. He'd been operational himself, so knew exactly how the public (or police) can easily put two and two together and calculate five.

However, the manager was dissatisfied with the police officer's accusations, attitude and hostility towards us, and so he asked Dale to share the voice recording with him. He explained to us that he intended to write an official letter of complaint to the constabulary, including the dialogue from the recording.

Several weeks went by before Dale and I were called into the station manager's office once again. He handed us a letter that he'd received from a senior officer in the constabulary's HQ. It contained an apology to Dale and I on behalf of the off-duty police officer involved, and also went on to explain, with words to the effect, that he'd been given a proper dressing down by a senior police officer.

PRF Audit Laughter

Punctuation: the bane of any author's career. It can change the entire meaning of a sentence, as too can spelling to some degree, as you'll see below.

While I was in the ambulance service, both as a paramedic clinical support officer, and also while full-time operational, mentoring students, I often audited PRFs to ensure that the correct drugs and drug dosages were documented, and that the appropriate assessments had been undertaken. In addition, I would check that an adequate and comprehensive set of notes were recorded, amongst a lot of other clinical details.

While undertaking a PRF audit, I wasn't interested in the paramedic's understanding of the English language, and it certainly wasn't my place to provide positive or negative feedback. Having said that, I did occasionally come across some very funny examples of poor spelling, grammar or punctuation and couldn't help but chuckle to myself, along with the authors of the PRFs themselves at times.

Case in point: the following sentences were taken from real patients' documentation recorded by a variety of paramedics from three different NHS ambulance services.

This first example of misspelling had me and my mentee in tears of laughter, after I'd pointed out their mistake and allowed him to complete the PRF without my supervision. Obviously, I can't publish the entire passage here, merely the few pertinent words from the PRF. It said the following:

1. *PCO/ (that's 'patient complains of') A saw foot after tripping up the stairs yesterday. Patient elevated his leg but to very little relief and his foot still remains saw.*

I only spotted the above mistakes while checking my mentee's completed PRF prior to handing the carbon copy over to the nurse, and, therefore, I chose not to ask him to re-write the whole PRF again.

This next one involves a punctuation mistake which could be perceived by many as completely changing the history of events. The additional information started like this:

2. *PCO/ Pain in the neck after hanging himself. a wall clock and over-reaching while trying to link the clock's catch onto the picture hook.*

That simple 'full-stop' after *'himself'* changes the perceived presenting complaint entirely!

3. *PCO/ Unable to move after the dog bit his own backside.*

Why on earth wouldn't you be able to move after a dog had bitten its own bum? What I think the clinician meant to say is:

PCO/ Unable to move after the dog bit his owner's backside.

Even assuming that was what the clinician had intended to say, it still doesn't make any sense to me whatsoever!

4. *PCO/ Headache and chest pain in the upper back.*

Hey? I was bamboozled!

5. *PCO/ Swollen jaw after being assaulted by a dog's pore.*

Not only is there a spelling mistake, but what on earth went on here I don't know!

6. *PCO/ Sudden onset of shortness of breath while going aboot his bizness.*

Obvious misspellings, and I can only assume that this particular clinician was Scottish.

7. *PCO/ Severe pain in the rectum while sat on the toilet for the*

last 3 weeks the patient has seen his GP twice due to piles/haemorrhoids. Possibly a fisher.

What I think the clinician meant to say is:

PCO/ Severe pain in the rectum while sat on the toilet. For the last 3 weeks the patient has seen his GP twice due to piles/haemorrhoids. Possibly a fissure.

The clinician who completed the following paper PRF obviously had an OCD about correct spelling, because they drew lines through their multiple attempts at writing what I call 'rusty bum wee':

8. *PCO/ Severe ~~diahorea diahorrea diahorrae~~ diarrhoea and headache.*

I have to admit, I always had to concentrate hard when spelling the word diarrhoea, when completing my clinical records.

9. *PCO/ Contraptions 5 minutes apart. Patient is full-term plus 2 days.*

The former wasn't an isolated case. I've seen the word contraptions, as opposed to contractions, written on many, many PRFs during my career.

10. *PCO/ Severe pain in chest. Also CO/ Pain in back both front and centre for the last several hours.*

I guess this clinician needs a refresher in human anatomy, hey!

The above examples are just a small selection of my favourite sentences from the countless PRFs I've had the pleasure of auditing. We all make mistakes, that's why there's little erasers on the end of pencils, why ink erasers exist, and also why I hired copy-editor, Kevin O'Byrne, to professionally edit and proofread this book, along with my previous three books!

ACHOO

Throughout their day-to-day or night-to-night roles, NHS personnel, both clinical and non-clinical, are frequently exposed to airborne viruses, diseases, bacterial infections, etcetera. At the time of recalling and writing this next story, the population of the United Kingdom is enduring its second *Covid-19* lockdown. With the exception of the Coronavirus, NHS personnel tend to develop very strong immune systems because of their heightened exposure, via airborne droplets or other fluid contact, to patients with a wide variety of transmittable infections.

This next incident involves just that, my own exposure to droplet-form bacteria from a patient experiencing severe hay fever, repeatedly sneezing while I attended to her. Fortunately for me, this incident occurred a long time before the Coronavirus pandemic.

Paramedic, Gabby, and I were on a day shift, one beautiful, hot summer's day. The environmental Celsius temperature was in the high twenties, and the pollen count was very high. We were ambling along in the ambulance, chatting away, when an emergency call was passed to us. We were dispatched to attend to a forty-odd year-old lady who was experiencing severe hay fever and the related signs of itching, streaming eyes and frequent episodes of repeated sneezing.

When we arrived at the patient's bedside, it became apparent that she was suffering considerably. She'd gone through multiple boxes of tissues; her eyes were bright red and looked saw. Ha-ha, I jest! Her eyes looked sore and she was furiously scratching her nose, eyes and arms. She was slightly short of breath but was able to converse with us, and so I ascertained that her name was Marie.

Gabby and I began assessing Marie and undertook a set of vital observations. Our concern was the severity of her condition and, consequently, we advised her to visit A&E for further observations and a doctor's clinical opinion. We were concerned her condition could deteriorate beyond straightforward hay fever; for example, to anaphylaxis. That's rare with hay fever, but not impossible. I have to say it was the worst case of hay fever that I'd ever seen.

Feeling empathy towards Marie, Gabby and I agreed it would be best if we saved the patient from having to walk to the ambulance, and so chose to use the carry-chair. Her Sp02 reading was at 98%, so no supplemental oxygen was necessary, nor clinically appropriate. Gabby went to fetch the carry-chair from the ambulance, while I stayed with Marie.

Up to this particular point, Marie had only sneezed a few times in our presence. But while conversing with her, I witnessed Marie have a severe bout of repetitive sneezing. Consequently, I began pondering about the potential health and safety issues of carrying her down the stairs.

Gabby returned with the carry-chair and Marie sat herself onto it. We securely strapped her in, including her arms. That is done to prevent the patient reaching out to grab anything, particularly the stair handrail or banister, as this can be dangerous for both the patient and the crew carrying them.

Still pondering, I decided to ask Marie whether she would mind wearing an oxygen mask, to contain any droplets if she began sneezing as we descended the stairs. She initially obliged to wearing one, but after I'd placed it onto her face, she very quickly felt suffocated, almost claustrophobic. I reluctantly removed it from her face and, given Marie's reluctance to tolerate an oxygen mask, made the decision that Gabby and I should wear one instead, obviously without supplemental oxygen flow.

Now Marie was in position and securely sat on the carry-chair, Gabby wheeled her out of the bedroom, along the landing, and stopped at the top of the stairs. I positioned myself on the first stair and took hold of the foot end of the carry-chair.

"One, two, three, lift," I said to Gabby. We began to descend the stairs, taking each step carefully. Marie, however, had another sneezing episode. I counted about twelve sneezes. Marie sounded like she was enjoying each sneeze. To be fair, sneezing is quite therapeutic, maybe even orgasmic!

That reminds me of a funny joke I remember being told; I've adopted my own version of the joke to avoid plagiarism. It goes like this:

A husband and wife were sitting beside each other in the first-class section of an aeroplane.

The woman sneezed, took out a tissue, gently wiped her nose, and then visibly shook in pleasure for ten to fifteen seconds. Her husband went back to his reading.

A few minutes later, the woman sneezed again, took a tissue, wiped her nose, then shook violently once more.

Assuming his wife might have a common cold, he thought little of it but was curious about the shaking.

A few more minutes passed when the woman sneezed yet again. As before, she took a tissue, wiped her nose, her body shaking even more than before.

Unable to restrain his curiosity, he turned to his wife and said,

"I couldn't help but notice that you've sneezed three times, wiped your nose and then shaken quite violently, darling. Are you OK?"

"I am sorry if I disturbed you, darling. I don't know what is the matter. Whenever I sneeze I have an orgasm," she said. Her husband, quite concerned, said,

"Well, what are you going to do about it, see the GP when we get home?" he asked.

"No," his wife replied. "I'm going to buy a wholesale amount of ground pepper!"

Anyway, as we descended the stairs, Gabby and I wearing oxygen masks as protective shields, Marie continued sneezing repeatedly. I had to endure watching the spray of droplets enter the atmosphere, primarily towards my face. It was disgusting, but I said nothing. Gabby was laughing out loud, causing her to steam up her mask! Marie was laughing too, and continuously apologised for her bacteria-infested, snotty episodes. I was periodically stopping on the stairs, bringing the carry-chair to a resting halt and trying to shield my eyes with my sleeved arm.

As we reached the bottom of the stairs, we opened the front door, lifted the carry-chair over the threshold and wheeled Marie towards the ambulance. Great, you would think. Oh no. It just so happened that several people were walking past Marie's house...

They all found it very funny – and very odd – that Gabby and I, as the paramedics, were wearing oxygen masks, while Marie, the patient, wasn't!

Holey Harness

A significant part of my role as an experienced paramedic was to mentor: act as a third-party observer and supervise paramedics, for a wide variety of reasons. This next incident involved my best friend, Graham, and I.

We were on a twelve-hour day shift, accompanied by our fellow colleague, Julie. She was returning to paramedic duties following a period of maternity leave. The purpose of three of us 'manning' an emergency ambulance was to ensure that Julie still had the confidence to attend to a variety of patients with varying medical conditions. She was a brilliant paramedic, so Graham and I weren't concerned one iota about her returning to autonomous practice. However, for her welfare, and professional registration purposes, it was necessary.

As a three-person crew, we were passed a routine call to convey a severely disabled lady from the care home, where she was a resident, into a hospital ward. Those type of calls are straightforward and simply involve the use of a hydraulic hoist, and a hammock type harness/sling to lift and move the patient from their bed to the stretcher.

We were welcomed by two care assistants as we entered the patient's room, introduced ourselves, and then Graham and I stood back and allowed Julie to attend to the patient and make all of the necessary decisions. What struck Graham and I almost immediately on entering the room, was that one of the care assistants had a severe case of a condition called strabismus. There are many variances, but to keep it simple, it means crossed-eyed, boss-eyed, boz-eyed, gozzy-eyed, to name but a few of the several well-known slang terms for the condition. This particular care assistant's eyes met each other in the middle, as if she was looking for the bridge of her own nose!

Now, have you ever been talking to someone and they look like they're talking to somebody stood behind you? I have, on several occasions, both on and off duty. The first time it happened to me I was off-duty, stood queuing in a newsagent, holding a magazine to purchase. When I reached the front of the queue, the cashier said, "Can I help?" One of her eyes was looking at me and the other was looking past me! Confused, I glanced over my shoulder, but there was nobody there. I then looked back at the cashier and replied,

"Oh, me? Sorry, love." I felt blood rush to my cheeks because of the feeling of guilt and embarrassment. Though I'm sure she must have been used to people doing the same 'over the shoulder glance' day in, day out.

On another occasion, I was in a very important meeting accompanied by my peers and some of my superiors. Sat before us were several NHS managerial staff. One of them, a lady, had the same condition - strabismus - though it wasn't *blatantly* obvious. My boss, sat a few feet away from me, asked her a question, but while she answered his question, her gaze was directed at me. Consequently, I interrupted her, pointed my finger at my boss and said, "He asked you the question, not me."

All of my peers in the room looked at me as if to say, 'Are you taking the piss, Andy?!' Then, realising she must have an unfortunate eye condition, I and several others covered our mouths with our hands in an attempt to stop ourselves from laughing at my unintended insult!

Anyway, moving on. Julie liaised with the care assistants and requested the hydraulic hoist and a harness. While one of the care assistants went to fetch the equipment, Julie carried on asking the one who had strabismus some more questions on the patient's past medical history. Graham and I continued observing, therefore allowing Julie to make the decisions necessary to transfer the patient from her bed to the stretcher. Moments later, the care assistant returned with the hoist.

They placed the hoist in the appropriate position, then Julie asked Graham to untangle the sling, ready to place under the patient. Stood next to Graham, I looked on, observing Julie. Graham unfolded the sling in its entirety and held it fully open, with both arms held high. To Julie and the care assistants, his face was hidden by the sling. However, *some* hoist slings are designed with very small holes in the material.

To my alarm, Graham, still holding the sling up, turned his head to look at me, deliberately crossed his eyes, and stuck out his tongue! I held my hand over my mouth and then discreetly whispered, "Stop it, there's holes in it. She'll see you."

Regardless, Graham kept lowering the sling, displaying a serious expression, then raised it again and pulled the same crossed-eyed, tongue out, facial contortion at me. He did that repeatedly until Julie asked him to pass her the sling. I was itching to leave the room so I could burst out laughing!

Once the patient was safely secured on the stretcher, we wheeled her out of the care home and into the ambulance. Graham and I sat in the cab, leaving Julie to complete the paperwork. We were in absolute stitches en route, and Julie eventually popped her head through the sliding window into the cab to ask what was making us laugh so much. Still laughing, I gave a hand sign to indicate that I'd tell her later.

I waited until after Julie had handed over the patient to the ward nurse, before explaining what Graham had been doing in the patient's room. Julie gave a wide-eyed expression of disbelief and let out a loud laugh.

I daren't publish them all, but Graham and I got into a lot of humorous situations while working together. Working with Graham provided, without a doubt, some of the best and funniest times I ever experienced throughout my career in the ambulance service.

A Pain in the Arse

Ambulance personnel frequently attend to patients with ailments and conditions that they're unable to really do anything about, other than refer the patient to their own GP, other healthcare professional, or offer self-care advice. This is partly due to the patient's complaint or condition not being strictly an accident or an emergency.

I remember being dispatched, along with my crewmate, to a twenty-six year-old woman complaining of bleeding from her vagina, known as 'bleeding per vagina' (PV bleed) to medical personnel. Obviously, vaginal bleeding can be very serious, potentially requiring invasive pre-hospital treatment, followed by in-hospital treatment. On the other hand, it could be related to menstruation, or another non-serious condition.

When my crewmate and I arrived inside the patient's lounge, the patient immediately jumped to her feet from the sofa, pulled down her leggings and knickers, and shouted, "Look, it's still bleeding!" Shocked, surprised and unprepared for a display of such hirsute genitalia, and also the abundance of philosophical phrases tattooed on her body, I didn't know whether to first read her and then react, or vice-versa! Of course, my immediate response was to say,

"Whoa, whoa, whoa! Put your hairy growler away, love! Gordon bloody Ramsey, I'm not a gynaecologist!"

In other incidences, often while parked up on stand-by, I would be approached by members of the public who would ask me for advice relating to skin conditions, eyesight issues, muscle complaints, minor cuts and bruises, and marital problems – even extra-marital problems!

I specifically remember being approached by a gentleman while I was working solo on an RRV. During my afternoon nap, waiting for a call to be passed to me, he knocked on the driver's side window, and while I thought, 'how rude of him, interrupting my nap', I wound down the window.

"Have you got an Elastoplast please, mate?" he asked.

"No, my friend, I haven't, sorry."

He looked at me with surprise and said, "What, you're a paramedic and you don't carry plasters?" I gave him a friendly smile and replied,

"This is an accident and emergency vehicle. If you were a treble-nine caller and the only treatment you required was an Elastoplast, then you should never have called treble-nine in the first place. That's why we're not equipped with them."

"Fair point," he answered. "I never thought of it like that."

In this next incident, Izzie and I were crewed together on a twelve-hour day shift. It was early afternoon and ambulance dispatch made contact via our cab radio.

"Go ahead, over."

"Roger. Urgent call for you to attend to a thirty-year-old female experiencing severe rectal pain, over."

Izzie began mobilising in the direction of the address, without blue lights. Urgent and routine calls do not justify the use of blue lights and sirens, whereas calls coded as RED are triaged as serious or potentially life-threatening.

While en route, my good friend, Dan, rang me on my mobile phone. "Hi, buddy. How are you?" he asked.

"I'm fine, cheers. We're just on our way to a pain in the arse," I replied.

"What, a frequent caller?"

"No, no. Literally a woman with a pain in her arse. We're just rolling up on scene now. I'll have to go."

When we arrived inside the patient's house, paramedic response bag in hand, Izzie and I were presented with a young lady sat on her sofa. I introduced us both to the patient and then ascertained that her name was Sam. I sat myself down beside her on the sofa. Meanwhile, Izzie placed the large paramedic bag onto the carpeted floor and sat herself down precariously on the bag, opposite Sam.

Using the paramedic bag as a seat was – maybe still is – common-place amongst ambulance personnel. It's reasonably comfortable, though height-wise it's a bit like sitting on a chair in an infant school classroom; your knees tend to be almost level with your chin!

My initial thought was that Sam appeared to be rather tense; she was almost hovering her backside off the sofa. 'Haemorrhoids' sprung to mind. Izzie was thinking the same, too. While Sam's eyes were directed at me, Izzie lip-synced the word 'piles' to me.

I began to question Sam as to what her concerns were. "So, Sam. Why have you rung for an ambulance today, then?" I asked.

"Well, I was sat down watching TV, then all of a sudden I got this horrendous, sharp, shooting pain up my bum, right up the tailbone," she explained. Her description didn't sound like the typical signs and symptoms of haemorrhoids, but maybe an after-effect of having suffered with haemorrhoids. I continued questioning her.

"Do you have, or have you ever experienced haemorrhoids, or piles as you may know it?"

"I've had them in the past," Sam replied, "but I don't have piles now. This was a sudden, sharp, horrendous shooting pain. It was awful. I've never had it before."

Izzie had remained mute so far. She was just sat, relaxed on the paramedic bag. I continued questioning further, generally asking questions with reference to stress, any problems related to her rectum, coccyx (tailbone), etcetera. My differential diagnoses were conditions called Proctaglia Fugax, or Levator Ani Syndrome.

With the exception of undertaking a set of vital observations, there wasn't a lot I could do for Sam. A visit to her own GP was looking like a more appropriate option. There, if deemed serious or absolutely necessary, a referral for her to see a colorectal surgeon for further assessment could be arranged by her GP.

With that in mind, I began explaining my diagnostic thoughts and plan of action to Sam. However, while doing so, she suddenly screamed and shot up off the sofa, stood in an almost rigid-like manner, and reached her arm round to the crack of her bum as if she'd been stabbed in the arse with a red-hot poker! Startled, Izzie simultaneously fell backwards off the parabag, legs akimbo in the air as if performing a pathetic attempt at junior school gymnastics!

I immediately burst out laughing, as too did Izzie. Sam, however, simply apologised to Izzie for her sudden movement, and said, "See what I mean? That's what's been happening every twenty minutes!"

After composing myself, but still chuckling, I said, "It could be what I told you, Sam, the condition called Proctaglia Fugax. If I make a GP appointment for you today, the GP may offer you a prescription for a muscle relaxant. Don't worry, though, Proctaglia Fugax is quite a common problem, and women are more susceptible to it."

I completed the paperwork and then contacted Sam's GP and explained my medical thoughts to her. Subsequently, the GP consulted with Sam and arranged an appointment for the same day.

Occasionally, throughout the rest of the shift, I'd visualise Sam shooting up off the sofa and Izzie falling backwards off the parabag, legs akimbo in the air, and I'd chuckle to myself.

Language Barrier

As an Englishman, I speak fluent English. I also speak a little Polish, because my partner is Polish, so she's taught me some of the lingo. In addition to those languages, I'm currently learning Geordie and Glaswegian at night college. I jest!

This next incident, involving me and my best friend, Graham, proved to be quite a challenge from a language point of view, but nevertheless, hilarious!

We were on a day shift, roaming the streets in the ambulance, when a call was passed to us by the dispatcher. The call was to attend to a twelve-year-old boy who was experiencing abdominal pain. He was on a school trip all the way from Russia. He was accompanied by one of his teachers, who was also Russian. The only information we were given of the whereabouts of the patient was that he was sat on a bench near the High Street. Graham mobilised towards town and, by some miracle, we found the patient and his teacher in a timely manner.

I introduced Graham and I, then welcomed them both on board the ambulance. I began my attempts at questioning the young lad while he lay, semi-recumbent, on the stretcher. His teacher sat herself on a chair beside him. Graham began undertaking some basic observations.

Now, we assumed – which you should never do, because *'to assume will make an ass-of-u-&-me'* – that because they were visiting England from Russia, then they probably spoke some English. Yes, they did... they could both say 'Huh?'

With the four of us in the saloon of the ambulance, I asked the young schoolboy, "Can you point with one finger where the pain in your tummy is?" He looked at me with confusion, then looked at his teacher with confusion, and his teacher looked at me with confusion.

"Huh?" she said.

'This could prove very difficult,' I thought. While Graham continued undertaking the patient's blood pressure, blood sugar levels, etcetera, I attempted to question further.

"Can you tell me how painful your tummy is?" I asked. Once again, a look of confusion was evident on his face, and his teacher's face, too. The teacher then began to speak to him in Russian. To Graham and I, it sounded like sheer gobbledygook. It might as well have been Swahili, Glaswegian, or Geordie! We didn't have a clue. I tried once more.

"Have you been able to wee normally?" I asked.

"Huh?" the boy uttered, and once again, that same look of confusion on both of their faces.

"Wee-wee!?" I said. Graham and I looked at each other and let out spontaneous sighs. Then Graham spoke up,

"I know, let's try charades." He placed both of his hands next to his trouser zip, simulating being stood at the toilet, then moved his hips from left to right, uttering, "pssssssss, pssssssss, pssssssss."

"Fireman Sam!" I said, laughing.

Graham put his thumb up to the boy. In Russian, his teacher must have then said something along the lines of, 'Are you able to wee-wee?' Moments later, he returned the gesture with a thumbs-up to me.

"Nice one, mate," I said to Graham. Then, returning my attention to the boy, I asked, "Have you been able to poo normally?" A further look of confusion, accompanied by,

"Huh?"

Graham put a hand behind his own backside, stuck out his tongue

120

and let out several raspberry blows to simulate going for a poo, albeit a noisy one! Well, that immediately had both Graham and I cracked up in laughter and bent over in stitches!

Difficult to imagine what the boy's teacher must have thought of us, but speaking in Russian she must have then said something along the lines of, 'Are you able to poo?' The young lad gestured a thumbs-up once more. I then asked, while rubbing my stomach,

"Do you feel sick, or have you been sick at all?" I simulated retching and loudly vomiting. His teacher then asked him a question, and he shook his head, so I took it that he had no nausea or vomiting.

After a further ten minutes of humorous, charade-like simulations as an aide to asking relevant clinical questions, along with using a FLACC scoring scale that shows emoji-like cartoon faces – usually only used in children aged two to seven – we were able to ascertain enough information from the young Russian schoolboy.

It was decided it warranted a visit to A&E, accompanied by his teacher. There, I'm sure they would have been able to track down the services of a Russian speaking translator, or perhaps a telephone translation service, to ascertain the young Russky's symptoms, and therefore diagnose and treat him accordingly.

Home Time

This next incident involved a long-serving (now retired) paramedic and former colleague of mine, who I liked and respected dearly. He had a fantastic – and sick – sense of humour, and was so laid-back that his nickname should have been 'Horizontal'. I'm not going to mention here what his real nickname is, instead I'm going to call him Del, for the purpose of this story.

He and his regular crewmate always had a great laugh working alongside each other, and experienced some very funny incidents. Case in point: this following incident involved a twenty-odd year-old patient called Phil, and his accompanying, similarly aged friend, Rob. The nature of the patient's ailments that caused him to ring treble-nine is irrelevant to the story; what is relevant is the humorous conclusion. It's only a short story, but nevertheless funny in my and many other people's opinion.

Del and Ken were approaching the end of their 7am until 7pm shift, and they'd been busy throughout the whole day and, therefore, keen to get off-duty on time. En route to A&E, Phil sat comfortably on board the ambulance, with his friend, Rob, sat nearby. Del began completing his paperwork in the saloon, while also engaging in conversation with both Phil and Rob about the day-to-day role of a paramedic; shift times, salary, etcetera. Meanwhile, Ken sat in the driver's seat, tootling along, oblivious to anything that was being said.

Arriving outside the A&E entrance at approximately 6:35pm, all four of them entered the reception area and Del handed over the patient to the duty triage nurse.

At approximately 6:45pm, Del vacated the ward and returned to the ambulance. Ken was talking to another crew close by. Moments later, Rob approached Del, smoking a cigarette, and engaged in conversation with him. That conversation went something like this:

Rob: "So what do you guys do now, clear and get sent to another call?"

Del: "No, mate. We're off at seven, so we'll just hang around here for a bit."

Rob: "Can they not pass you another emergency if it'll mean you'll finish late, then?"

Del: "Oh yeah, of course they can."

Rob: "How come you're not going to another emergency now, then?"

Del: "Because we want to finish on time, and get home and drink a four-pack."

Rob: "Yeah but they might have another patient desperate for an ambulance."

Del: "That's just it, mate. They will have, and we'll probably cop for it if we clear now. It's just not worth the risk."

Rob: "Well what if somebody has been waiting ages for an ambulance? You're available now."

Del: "They'll still get an ambulance. The nightshift will be on-duty by now, so they'll get the call."

Rob: "That's disgraceful, that is. You could be responding to another call right now, though."

Del: "Listen, mate. It's nearly seven o'clock. If we clear now, they'll pass us another treble-nine and we won't get home until eight-thirty, maybe nine o'clock. Plus, we're back in at seven in the morning. We have lives and a family too, you know. We do sixty-hours a week as it is. If we finished late after every shift, we'd be working seventy or more hours per week. We're only human. We can't save the world all by ourselves."

Ken then returned from talking to the other ambulance crew, and approached Del and Rob still conversing.

Ken: "What time is it, Del?"

Del: "Two minutes to seven."

Ken: "Right, come on, let's get ready to clear."

Rob: "I can't believe you two. You're waiting 'til seven so they can't pass you a further emergency call?"

Ken: "Yeah. What's the problem?"

Del: "He seems to think we don't have lives, or should want to call it another day and another measly dollar. Instead, he thinks we should clear before seven o'clock and stay on longer."

Ken: "B*****ks to that!"

Rob: "Well, I think you're both bang out of order."

On that comment, Del looked directly at Rob, stuck his tongue out and let out a huge, over-exaggerated and long-winded raspberry blow, as if to say, 'I don't care what you think, so there!' Ken had a good old belly laugh at Del's cheeky response, and they both boarded the ambulance.

As by now it had turned seven o'clock, they cleared with control and proceeded back to the ambulance station, allowing them to finish their shift *almost* on time.

Walking Wounded

This next story involved a road traffic collision involving several cars and a coach-load of passengers. It was declared as a major incident due to the number of potential casualties, not because of the seriousness of the incident; fortunately, no serious injuries or deaths occurred. But if you've previously worked, or still work, in any of the emergency services, then I'm sure you'll have experienced some humorous occurrences even while on scene at major or time-critical incidents.

There were multiple casualties in this particular incident, and while most of them had only minor injuries, a lot of vehicles from all three emergency services were present. The fire service was undertaking its role, the police had cordoned off the scene, and the ambulance service was dealing with the most prioritised of casualties.

Where does the humour come in to all this? Well, as you are probably aware, ambulances have a back door entrance/exit which opens up as a ramp to load and off-load patients, and also a sliding side door on the nearside of the vehicle. Try to visualise this: One particular crew, Brian and Kevin, were dealing with a patient laid on the stretcher in the saloon of their vehicle, with both the back door and side door open. Stood outside of their ambulance, near the open back door, was a police officer.

While Brian assessed and treated his significantly injured patient, the copper was beckoning the walking wounded to step aboard the ambulance in order to receive treatment for their minor injuries. This was despite him knowing that Kevin and Brian were already dealing with a priority patient. However, unbeknown to the copper, Kevin was immediately asking them to step back off the ambulance through the open side door!

I assume it must have prompted the transiting minor wounded to scratch their heads and ask what was the point in being prompted by the copper to step aboard the ambulance for treatment, only to be asked to step straight back out through the side door! As for the copper, he must have been surprised and impressed at the capacity of the saloon, or Brian and Kevin's speedy turnaround service!

Frequent Caller

Globally, every single frontline employee of the emergency ambulance service will have, without a doubt, responded to an abundance of 'frequent callers' during their career; it's inevitable! I'm not talking about those who ring 999, 112 or 911 several times per month. Oh no, that's acceptable if genuinely warranted and they accept the advice and/or treatment offered. I'm talking about those people who ring and request an ambulance response several times *per day...* and demand that a paramedic attend their address or location immediately!

This next incident involved a frequent caller that *almost all* personnel, from the ambulance station I was working from at the time, had attended to on many occasions. So much so that nearly all had become well-known to the patient, and vice-versa, and the patient was on first name terms with each crew member. I, on the other hand, had never had the 'pleasure' – I say that with intended sarcasm – of meeting him. That was about to change when Dave and I were passed his name and address one particular evening while on a nightshift.

The cab radio alarmed. "Go ahead, over."

"Roger, RED call. You're responding to a twenty-five year-old male complaining of shortness of breath. You're the fifth crew to attend within the last twenty-four hours, over!" the despatcher said with exclamation in her voice.

"Roger, going mobile, over," I replied.

While Dave drove to the address, he explained to me that he'd been called to the patient, Gavin, on countless occasions. He also explained how the patient has a different medical complaint every time he rings treble-nine, and also that he insists that he's blind! He went on to tell me that Gavin is rude and can get hostile and aggressive, and always refuses to go to hospital, regardless of the numerous offers of help for his ailments and *alleged* blindness.

Arriving inside Gavin's studio flat, we found him laid in bed. My first impression was that he was extremely unkempt in appearance. He had long, straggly, scruffy hair and a long, scruffy beard. Evidently not an avid fan of hygiene or house cleaning, it's fair to say that the place was an absolute tip! Mental health problems sprung to mind.

Gavin immediately recognised Dave and so greeted his presence on first name terms. I, however, introduced myself, before Dave began questioning his reasons for ringing treble-nine for the sixth time in twenty-four hours. I stood back, analysing Gavin for his mannerisms and body language. I also scanned his flat for any obvious hints and tips on why he was such a frequent caller and accepted living in squalor.

I found a huge pile of carbon-copy, non-conveyance forms left by an abundance of ambulance attendees. Scan-reading through them, I noticed the majority of staff who'd attended had noted that he was 'blind'... not registered blind, but nonetheless blind. I smelt a rat!

Looking at him, he didn't appear *obviously* blind, and he made *almost* normal eye contact while conversing. Furthermore, he certainly wasn't experiencing shortness of breath in any way whatsoever.

Keeping my cynicism to myself for a little longer, I undertook a full set of vital observations on him, while Dave continued to question further. Gavin was very chatty throughout – certainly not a sign of suffering any shortness of breath.

As time went on, and having read through quite a lot of the non-conveyance forms, I had a little wander round his flat, searching for clues. I picked up on a few inconsistencies related to his alleged blindness... but I decided to keep schtum for a little longer. I scanned his CD collection shelved on a bedside cabinet. 'Mmm,' I thought, 'let's see if he slips up'.

I pulled out a CD case of *Dire Straits – Brothers in Arms*, and commented, "Oh, I love this CD, Gavin. I have my own copy at home." Actually I didn't. "Which is your favourite song on here?" I asked, as I placed the reverse of the CD case in front of him.

"That one there, number five," he said, pointing his index finger directly at the fifth song title. With an expression of some confusion, Dave then spoke up.

"I thought you said—"

"No, no, Dave," I interrupted, "hold your thought, mate."

Gavin didn't realise what he'd done, or if he did then he thought we hadn't twigged his 'schoolboy error'. Dave gave me a subtle nod and we both chuckled, Gavin seemingly none the wiser as to why.

"So, you're blind, Gavin... is that right?" I asked. He looked almost directly at me and replied,

"Yeah, for five years now. I'm not registered blind though, or use a white stick, or have a guide dog or anything. I manage though, by holding my arms out and feeling about, you know." I scanned round the room once again and asked,

"Do you suffer with any mental health conditions, or take any antidepressants, at all?"

"No, never, and I don't take any medication," he answered. I pondered further, looked around the room again and mentally noted some more discrepancies.

"I take it you live alone, Gavin?" I asked.

"Yeah."

"Any carers, relatives or friends ever visit you at all, with you being blind?" I asked with an element of sarcasm in my tone.

"No, I just fend for myself. I'm happy living by myself, it's great. My friends live miles away and never come here."

"Um, I'm intrigued, Gavin. You tend to call the ambulance service a lot... several times a day actually, but you always refuse to go to A and E. Why is that?"

"I don't like hospitals. You guys tend to treat me at home," came his response. I smelt an even bigger rat by now.

"Gavin, according to all those non-conveyance forms on the sideboard there, no crew has ever provided any treatment. They've all simply assessed you and found no medical concerns whatsoever. They offered to convey you for further assessment and a second opinion on each occasion, but historically you've always refused."

"Yeah, I'm happy and feel better when the paramedics have been and assessed me. It gives me peace of mind."

"Ah, I see. As for the blindness, can you explain to me why you could point directly at your favourite song on that CD I showed you?"

"I just know from the size of the CD case where number five is," he answered, causing Dave and I to grin to each other.

"What are you smiling for?" he asked.

"How d'ya know we're smiling?" I retorted.

"It's an acquired skill that blind people obtain over time," he replied, causing Dave and I to laugh out loud.

"Really? OK, can you explain why there's a dartboard hung on the wall with darts in the number nineteen, twenty and the bullseye? Have you been playing 'round the board' by yourself?"

"No, no," he answered, "they've been in the board since before I went blind."

"You also have an amateur darts trophy that you won just four years ago, yet you say you've been blind for five years."

"Hey?" he uttered.

"Yeah, I've just been admiring it. You're amazing, winning a pub darts tournament as a blind person. Oh, and a few other observations I've made that give me the impression you need some professional help."

"What are they?" he asked nervously.

"Your computer is showing the BBC News webpage."

"Is it? Somebody must've been using my computer."

"Really?" I replied with a chuckle. "You said no carers, relatives or friends come here." No response was heard from Gavin. "You also have newspapers and magazines strewn all over the place; none of them in Braille, by the way!"

"I've never read them, I can't see," he said with certainty.

"You also have a large poster of *Little Mix* on your wall... are all their naughty bits in Braille by any chance?" I asked with a smile on my face.

"Is there? I've never seen it, plus I don't like *Little Mix*."

Looking at me, Dave remarked, "Of all the times I've been here, I've never once stopped to look around, never noted clues like that, and none of the others have ever mentioned it either... probably because of the state of the place, to be fair." Turning to face Gavin, and in a stern voice, he said, "Gavin, look me in the eyes and tell me you're truly blind."

"Yeah, I am."

"Really?! Be truthful, because you've been abusing the purpose of the NHS emergency ambulance service several times a day, almost every day for several months now! You're not blind at all, are you?!" Dave asked with an assertive tone of voice. Knowing him well, I could only assume that he wasn't genuinely angry, more performing an act of amateur dramatics, and probably wanting to burst into laughter. But maybe he was genuinely pissed off with Gavin; I never did ask him.

"Well... not blind as in 'blind, blind', no. I sometimes have to wear my glasses."

"What type of glasses?" I asked.

"Reading glasses."

Dave and I grinned at each other once again. I could only assume we were both having the same thought, which was, 'Let's complete the one-millionth non-conveyance form and get out of here ASAFP! There's somebody out there who may genuinely need an ambulance.'

After further conversation with Gavin, during which he refused our offer of the opportunity to travel to A&E for a mental health assessment, or accept a professional referral to seek his GP, Dave quickly completed the paperwork. An additional carbon-copy was added to Gavin's growing collection of non-conveyance paperwork. We then left him in the comfort of his home and vacated the property.

Arriving back at the station, Dave explained the incident of the frequent caller to the station manager. Eventually, an official notice was disseminated to all staff, with words to the effect of 'do not fall for Gavin's alleged blindness'.

Following that official notice, Gavin's abuse of the ambulance service continued for a couple more months. Then, by some miracle, Gavin suddenly stopped ringing treble-nine, and nobody attended to him again. Several months later, my colleagues and I found out why.

As the rumour mill relayed it, he'd moved to another county, and senior managers of that county ambulance service had liaised with senior managers from our locality. It seems Gavin took all of his PRF carbon-copies with him to his new address, and an attending crew, after noting his previous address, had reported the abuse of the service.

But this only came after the paramedics working within the geographical area of Gavin's new address had, several times per day, every day for weeks, been attending to a twenty-five-year-old man who claimed to be blind! Until eventually a crew was not convinced that he was!

What Are the Chances?

This following tale is a short one, but I'm sure it will, at the very least, cause you to raise a smile.

My former colleague, Ian, an experienced paramedic, was working solo on an RRV and had recently cleared from an address, having been the first healthcare professional on scene to attend to an elderly patient. The back-up crew had arrived at the property and were continuing with the patient's treatment, allowing Ian to be available for the next treble-nine call.

You may or may not be aware that government targets in England – at the time of writing – require that, upon a RED call being received by ambulance control, a First Person on Scene (FPoS) volunteer, an ambulance technician, or a paramedic should arrive at a patient's side within 8 minutes. Politics, hey! Easy for them! With that explained, I'll continue.

Ian was parked up on standby, ready to receive his next RED call. While stood outside of the RRV to have a cheeky smoke, his cab radio alarmed.

"Go ahead, over," he said to the dispatcher.

"Roger, Ian. RED call to three-hundred and fifty-three, Rodney Lane. Repeat, three-five-three Rodney Lane. It's a nine-delta-one RED cardiac arrest, over."

"Roger, going mobile, over," he replied, and immediately moved to sit in the driver's seat of the RRV. But something suddenly dawned on him. He looked over his shoulder at the address behind him... and noticed that he was parked directly outside of three-five-three, Rodney Lane. What are the chances of that?!

Within ten or fifteen seconds of receiving the RED call, he replied to the dispatcher, "On scene, over." He quickly grabbed the necessary equipment and, with great haste, ran down the garden pathway and was met at the door by the caller.

"Good grief, that was quick!" she remarked, though clearly upset and panic-stricken.

Ian immediately proceeded to the patient... only to find that he wasn't in cardiac arrest at all; he'd fainted and experienced a brief episode of unconsciousness. With the panic over, Ian turned to the lady and eased her concerns.

The now relieved lady said to Ian, "You got here so fast, I don't know how you did it, but I'm impressed."

"We try our best, madam, and it's a bloody fast car."

A happy ending for the patient and his family, but also for Ian, who could boast about achieving the fastest ambulance service *'from call to arriving on scene'* response time since government targets began!

What a Rant

I must warn you that this next incident contains a lot of bad language, including the c-word... yes, *colourful*! I know most, not all, women hate hearing it and certainly do not use it as part of their daily vocabulary!

Jake, a technician, and I were working alongside each other on a Saturday nightshift. We were called to attend to a twenty-five year-old female who was under heavy influence of alcohol. Allegedly, she had become very aggressive towards other revellers at a house party. One of those revellers had rung treble-nine requesting an ambulance for medical support, and to remove her from the party.

Arriving at the address, Jake and I entered the property and were met by a crowd of 'tanked-up' party-goers, all of them aged around their mid to late twenties. We were escorted to the patient, who was situated in the lounge, screaming at other males and females present. Music was blaring out, so I immediately asked for the volume to be turned down. I didn't ask for it to be switched off completely, as I was enjoying the tune and didn't want to be a party-pooper!

Approaching the young lady, my first thought was that – tongue in cheek – she must have fallen out of the ugly tree and hit every single branch on the way down! Unbeknown to me at the time, that thought would be *voiced* later on that night.

Standing a few feet away from her, I was immediately met with a hostile attitude and an array of colourful language aimed specifically at *me*. Attempting to calm the situation, Jake asked other people present how much the patient had drank, and whether she had taken any recreational drugs. It became apparent that no drugs had been ingested, smoked, injected or snorted, but she had consumed quite a lot of alcohol. Under its influence, she was attempting to 'pick a fight', with both males and females, without any provocation whatsoever from any of them.

Refusing to get into any fisticuff situation with her, they'd chosen to ring for an ambulance, as opposed to the police. Likewise, I chose not to request police attendance, but instead attempted to use my charm to encourage and persuade her to leave the house party and allow us to escort her to the ambulance, where I could *attempt* to chat with her and assess her accordingly.

After time consuming persuasion, the patient voluntarily staggered and stumbled from the house, clambered into the ambulance, and slumped herself on the stretcher. As Jake then did his utmost best to obtain *some* vital observations, I began trying to ascertain her name, address, allergies, etcetera, with *some* success... I learned that her name was Jenny, that's it! As I began completing my paperwork – granted, there wasn't a lot to write down – Jenny roused and became quite vocal.

"W-where am I f**kin' goin', you tw*t?" she mumbled. "I wanna go home, you f**kin' c**t."

"Oi! Less of that, young lady!" I shouted.

Jake prepared to pin-prick her finger for a drop of blood, in order to measure her blood sugar level, which is a very important, pertinent medical test to undertake on a patient who is under the influence of alcohol. As he did, Jenny screamed out,

"Arrrgh! You c**t! What the f**k are you doing, you c**ting tw*t?!"

Laid on her side on the stretcher, she began to retch and spit a horrible, dry mucous onto the floor.

"Oi! Stop doing that, you filthy girl! That's disgusting!" I shouted.

"C**t off, you f**k," she replied, causing Jake and I to laugh at her reversed verbal barrage. Moments later, she vomited all over the floor of the ambulance, causing remnants of bile and fluid to splash on both mine and Jake's nicely polished boots.

Because of her behaviour, I asked Jake to place an oxygen mask onto her face, but not to administer any oxygen, as she didn't warrant it. A short time later, she became nauseous again and began retching, and attempted to sit herself up. Her very long hair had, for some unknown reason, become tangled around the metal mechanism of the stretcher. Before she had time to pull the oxygen mask from her face, she vomited inside it, causing it to fill up.

Jake and I couldn't help but laugh out loud, but I immediately pulled the mask from her face, causing more vomit to spill over the floor. I quickly untangled her hair from the stretcher. She sat up, her eyes partially closed and her face covered in vomit.

"Why the f**k did you tie my... my hair... to the, the bed, you t**t?"

"We didn't," Jake replied.

"You f**kin' did, you c**tin', f**kin' t**t," she mumbled. Jake and I chuckled at her ridiculous allegation. However, given all the colourful language that had left her mouth so far, I decided to request, via mobile phone, a private 'room', not the cubicle with a curtain that traditionally separates one A&E cubicle from another.

After the short journey, we arrived at A&E. Jenny had by now become a lot more roused, probably due to vomiting so much alcohol before it had chance to metabolise. Vacating the ambulance, Jake and I then wheeled Jenny, laid on her side on the stretcher, into the department.

Following a brief handover to Tiff, the triage nurse, I went to wash my hands. As I was doing so, I heard Jenny shouting at Cassie, the nurse charged with dealing with Jenny. "I wanna get out of here! I'm not f**kin' stayin' here, you bunch of c**ts!" she shouted.

I immediately went into the private room to provide support to Cassie and to help try to calm Jenny down. However, I was once again met by a barrage of expletives.

"You," she shouted, pointing her finger at me, "are a f**kin' c**t!"

"I beg your auntie and uncle pardon," I humorously replied whilst grinning, as I could see particles of vomit by now becoming a little encrusted on her face.

"Stop swearing!" said Cassie. "You're in A and E, and there's other poorly patients here too. They don't want to hear such appalling language, Jenny!"

Following that order from the nurse, Tiff and Dr Wang entered the private room. So there we all were, Tiff, Cassie, Dr Wang, Jake and I, all stood staring at Jenny sat on the bed, trying to calm her down. But with no joy; she ignored our attempts and instead spoke up abusively once again.

"Those f**kin' c**ts tied my hair to the stretcher, and made me hurl puke into a mask, the f**kin' c**ts!"

Moments later, the nurse intervened and said, "There's no need for such language, Jenny. Stop swearing and just lie down and be quiet, young lady."

"F**k off you fat, bearded bitch!" she replied, referring to the stubble-like facial hair on Cassie's chin. "And look at you," she said, directing her glare at Dr Wang, "you f**kin' slanty-eyed f**k, with your silver spoon hanging out your f**kin' mouth."

Tiff and Dr Wang were open-mouthed with shock at Jenny's insults. Jake and I deplored the racist insult especially, but we could only laugh at the state of her as she swayed side to side.

"Jenny, that'll do!" Tiff said sternly, "That's disgraceful, racist behaviour!"

"F**k the shut up, you... you stupid, fat, ugly, scruffy-haired bitch!"

Following that insult, Tiff left the room to contact security and request them to attend A&E.

Several minutes went by, and Jenny had shouted a further barrage of obscenities and insults at us, which Jake and I were still finding very funny coming from her. Tiff returned with two security guards, and the two middle-aged, semi-retired gents immediately received a mouthful of abuse from Jenny, too.

She stood up from the bed, staggering and swaying from side to side, and shouted, "You f**kin' bunch of c**ts! I f**kin' 'ate the f**kin' lot of you!"

I was stood there holding my hand over my mouth, trying not to laugh. You have to understand, we see and hear a lot of abuse and let most of it go over our heads. When you let that go and just look at the state of the patients delivering the abuse, it can be difficult not to laugh. But this time I was also thinking I'm not going to stand by and listen to her insult my professional peers, friends in fact, without giving her a little taste of her own medicine.

While looking at Jenny, and with a serious expression on my face, I said, "You know what? It's just dawned on me... I've been thinkin' of who you remind me of... It's just clicked."

Everybody in the room directed their eyes at me, wondering what I was going to say. "You're the absolute spittin' image of a bloke that lives near me... he's got a face like a bulldog licking piss off a nettle... actually, no, that's an insult to a bulldog. Your face is like a plate of moussaka that's been dropped and spilt all over the floor!"

I wanted to even the score a little, and following my witty, admittedly insulting comment, Jake, Tiff, Cassie, the two security guards, and even Dr Wang, all began laughing. But Jenny retaliated.

"F**k the shut up, you f**kin' cheeky b*****d! I look nothing like a bloke, you f**kin' big-eared, fat beer bellied c**t!"

"Oi... fuggly! I don't dispute that I'm a big-eared, big, fat, beer bellied c**t. But cheeky?" I retorted, "Me, cheeky? You're joking!"

"Fuggly? Look at you. I bet your mum's fat too, isn't she... you jug-eared t**t!" We all burst into laughter once again, as we'd all heard worse, and all of us were immune to it. I responded with,

"Oh, I see. Are we gonna have a 'your momma so fat' insult game, are we? Do you wanna start, or should I?"

"I'll f**kin' knock you out in a minute, I'll tell you that for free!" she replied.

"Really? For free? Why, how much do you usually charge?" I retorted.

Following Jenny's threat towards me, Tiff decided enough was enough and didn't want Jenny on the ward any longer. For a little while, the barrage of verbal abuse continued, and Jenny attracted more and more attention from other members of staff concerned about patients and their relatives in the nearby cubicles. The police were eventually called to attend.

Jenny was cautioned and arrested for being drunk and disorderly, then whisked off for a long night in 'hotel' custody. I call it karma, but I think Jenny must have called it excess alcohol consumption... after sobering up in the police cell, that is.

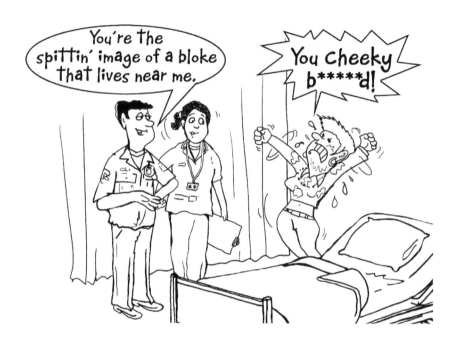

Discharge

This following incident happened many years ago, but I specifically remember it being recited to me only several years ago by a long-serving (now retired) ambulance man. He was one of the crew involved, and I've called him Bob throughout this short anecdote.

George and Bob, both ambulance technicians, were working alongside each other and were passed a routine call to convey a patient from a hospital ward, back to the care home where he was a permanent resident. The patient had been discharged by the doctor, and so required an ambulance to convey him safely home, under the supervision of medical personnel.

Arriving at the hospital entrance, Bob parked the ambulance, and then they both made their way to the ward, pushing the stretcher along a number of corridors. On the ward, a nurse escorted them to the patient, who she addressed as Harry. Bob asked Harry to lie, semi-recumbent, on the stretcher. Harry obliged, and then Bob placed some blankets over him and made him as comfortable as possible, ready for the short journey back to the care home.

After several minutes waiting for the patient's medication to be prepared and processed, and a further stroll back along the corridors, George and Bob arrived back at their ambulance. Carefully securing the stretcher in place, George sat himself down on a seat beside Harry. Bob then informed George that he was just going to nip to the loo before they began the journey to the care home. George acknowledged Bob's call of nature, so Bob slammed the back doors shut, ensuring that they were secured tight, and then made his way to the gents toilets.

Several minutes later, Bob returned and immediately adopted his position in the driver's seat. Starting the engine ignition switch, Bob shouted, "Moving off!" He ambled out of the hospital grounds and tootled along the roads in the direction of the care home.

After driving a mile or two, his cab radio sounded.

"Go ahead, over," said Bob.

"Roger, Bob. Can you turnaround and head back to the hospital, please?"

"What for?" he replied.

"To pick up your crewmate, George," the dispatcher answered.

Bob was obviously very confused by such a bizarre request, since only several minutes earlier he had shut the back doors of the ambulance with George sat inside. He proceeded to pull over on the roadside.

Peering into the saloon of the vehicle, he discovered the patient lying down, fast asleep, but his crewmate, George, was nowhere to be seen!

It turned out that after Bob had nipped to the loo, the patient then realised he'd left his reading glasses on the ward. George had vacated the ambulance and made his way back to the ward as quickly as he could, believing that he'd have time to retrieve the glasses and get back before Bob returned.

However, George's speedy bolt back to the ward wasn't quite speedy enough, and so upon Bob's return from the loo, he simply drove off and headed for the care home. Brilliant!

It wouldn't happen today, of course, because ambulance personnel should *never*, under any circumstances, leave their patient unattended in the ambulance.

Prank #2

If you enjoyed the earlier Prank #1 story, then I'm sure you'll enjoy this one, too. If, however, you thought it was sick and twisted, then I apologise profusely right now! But I know there are readers out there that love a good-ole 'sick and twisted' prank, so I decided to chance it and include the following in this book.

Luke, a rookie technician, and I were due to commence a twelve-hour day shift. Prior to arriving for duty, Luke dropped off his car at the vehicle auto centre for some repairs. The garage was only several minutes walk away from the local A&E and the ambulance station, so after leaving his car with the mechanics, he walked the rest of the way and arrived on time for his shift, crewed with me.

Luke was a really nice guy, possessed a great sense of humour, but was quite serious a lot of the time. I think he was still adapting to life in the ambulance service and what goes on... the banter, pranks, the dark sense of humour, and the quite laid-back attitude to life... and death!

By midday we'd already been quite busy, with very little time for refreshments. The treble-nine calls kept coming in and, before we knew it, it was 4pm. One quick brew and a couple of 'bickies' later, we were passed an urgent admission to convey a seventy-year-old patient from his home address and admit him into the nearby hospital.

Arriving inside the property, the patient, Jack, who had a proper Scouse accent – as opposed to a 'plastic Scouse' accent – informed us that he used to be an ambulance man. He'd served thirty-odd years during the days before paramedics even existed; they were only trained to provide very basic ambulance aid. However, even during his own career, a dark sense of humour and a lot of resilience was prevalent.

En route to hospital, with Luke driving and unable to hear our conversation, Jack asked me if we still played pranks on each other, similar to how they did during his career. Obviously I said we did, so Jack suggested that I play a prank on Luke, using him, the patient, as the subject of the prank. So, I did!

Arriving at the hospital, we vacated the ambulance and entered reception, wheeling Jack along the corridor to the ward. As I entered the ward, the nurse explained that they were not expecting Jack until around 7pm, and that there was no bed readily available for him yet. It was only 5pm, so we stood in the corridor with Jack still lying on the stretcher, chatting about the old days when he was in the service.

After twenty-odd minutes of waiting in the corridor, Luke asked, "Do you mind if I walk over to the garage and see if my car's ready, Andy?"

"Yeah, that's fine. We're probably going to be here a while yet," I replied. So off Luke went and headed to the garage, leaving me alone with Jack.

Ten minutes went by, and the nurse emerged from the ward and informed me that there was now a bed ready for Jack. I carefully wheeled him into the ward, assisted him to his bed, and then handed my PRF over to the nurse. I wished Jack all the best and wheeled the stretcher back into the corridor. There, I discarded the linen and placed it into the laundry bin, before re-covering the stretcher with fresh linen, ready for the next patient.

While waiting for Luke to return, I decided to grab a quick brew in the nurses' staff room, leaving the stretcher in the corridor. Having finished my cup of tea, I wandered back out and sat myself on the stretcher, waiting for Luke. Minutes later, Luke returned and met me along the corridor, noticing that Jack was no longer present.

"Oh, sorry Andy. I thought they didn't have a bed for him yet."

Placing an index finger over my lips, I said, "Shhh, keep your voice down. It went bad shortly after you left. How's your car, is it repaired?"

"Yeah, it's ready. What do you mean, it went bad after I left?"

I bowed my head to appear sombre and then said, "While I was stood in the corridor with him, he suddenly went into cardiac arrest. I had to shout for help from the corridor."

"You're joking!" Luke appeared shocked.

"Yeah, the nurse came bolting out of the ward and shouted for the crash team. She asked where my crewmate was. I just said you were in the loo."

Luke said nothing, so I continued. "It was awful, mate. He just went quiet. I checked his ABC's and he'd arrested. Me and the nurse quickly wheeled him into resus and started basic life support. The doctor asked where you were, he said the extra pair of hands would've made all the difference, and that he would have survived had you been here. But hey-ho, on a positive note, at least your car's fixed, hey!"

Luke's facial expression was a picture... a picture of guilt and devastation. "I feel awful, Andy. I'm not arsed about my car."

My mouth was aching. I wanted to burst into laughter and put him out of his misery from worrying about being absent during a cardiac arrest... but I didn't. Instead, I escalated the prank further!

I continued explaining what had happened during his absence.

"If it's any consolation to your sense of guilt, we did get him back at one point. He opened his eyes and said, 'Where's your mate? Tell him that I'm glad his car's repaired'. He must've been able to see you from heaven."

Luke shot me one of those looks; part disbelief, part anger, part relief. "What?! You're joking me! Are you winding me up? Is he OK?"

"Yeah, of course he is! Shortly after you'd left, the nurse allocated him a bed," I said.

"OMG! I felt absolutely devastated then! Shit, man!"

Laughing out loud, I replied, "Get used to it, buddy, you're in the ambulance service now. Expect the unexpected!"

To give Luke some *extra* peace of mind, we wandered back into the ward and approached Jack's bed. He was sat up, content and very comfortable. I explained to him what I'd done. Jack had a flamin' good belly laugh and, offering a high-five hand gesture, said,

"Nice one, lad! That's cheered me up!"

I wished Jack all the best, for a second time, and then Luke and I made our way back to the ambulance. There, we had a little chuckle together, and I could see the sense of relief on his face that it had only been a wind-up. Sick and twisted? Perhaps. Is it normal practice in the ambulance service? Absolutely!

Today's Challenge Is...

I've titled this next story 'Today's Challenge Is...' because there were times, depending on who I was working alongside, where we would set a humorous challenge to undertake while attending to our patients. Not, I hasten to add, those patients presenting with time-critical or life-threatening signs and symptoms. Only those who were non-time-critical or that we'd likely leave at home following a thorough assessment.

Commencing a day shift with my good friend and colleague, Jacob, we began checking our vehicle for adequate medical supplies, fresh batteries for the ECG machine, and so on, engaging in conversation along the way, when the subject of today's challenge arose.

"What d'ya fancy as today's challenge, Andy?" Jacob asked.

I thought for a moment. "Are you in the mood for song titles from the eighties?"

Jacob gave it a second's thought and nodded. "OK," he said, "that should be quite easy. I can see how that could be funny."

'Easy?' I thought, 'No chance,' but instead I replied, "That's agreed then."

The rules were that while questioning and assessing a patient, you had to bring in a song title from the 'eighties' without the patient realising any connection to our clinical questioning. The winner would be the one with the most song titles mentioned during the patient assessment, either while in the patient's home, or with both of us in the saloon of the ambulance with the patient. If a visit to A&E was warranted then scoring would cease as soon as one of us boarded the cab to drive.

Sat in the station mess room, waiting for our first call to be passed to us, I began thinking of eighties song titles that I could use during an assessment. Whether Jacob was pondering too, I don't know.

What became clear to me, though, is that it was actually a lot more difficult than you would think!

We attended to several patients within the first half of the shift, but all those calls were deemed inappropriate to undertake the challenge due to the patients' clinical signs and symptoms. However, later in the afternoon we were passed an urgent call to attend to an eighty-seven year-old female complaining of a sore foot.

Upon arriving in the patient's lounge, we found her lying on the sofa with both legs raised, and bare-footed.

"Good afternoon. I'm Andy, and this is *Ben*," I said.

"Oh, you cheeky... actually that doesn't count. That's a seventies song," Jacob stated.

"Doh! OK, it's still nil-nil then," I replied. The patient didn't have a clue what we were talking about, so I continued. "What's your name, my dear?" I asked as I knelt down next to her, opening up the equipment bag.

"Phyllis."

I began engaging in conversation with Phyllis while Jacob looked on. My initial impression was that she looked well, overall. Nothing alarming jumped out at me, so to speak. "I believe you have pain in your foot, is that right, Phyllis?" I asked. Remaining nice and relaxed on the sofa, she replied,

"Yes, my left foot." If her reply had been a song, and not the title of a classic movie starring Daniel Day Lewis, I'd have thought that Phyllis was playing along with us!

I was having a glance at Phyllis's left foot prior to commencing some vital observations, when all of a sudden Jacob cut in and, with a facial expression akin to a shriek, asked,

"Is the pain *Bad*, Phyllis?"

'Damn,' I thought, but replied, "Good one, mate!"

Now one-nil down, I had to carefully assess Phyllis further, while thinking of some corking questions and/or answers. "So, Phyllis, when did you last walk comfortably on your left foot?" I asked. Shuffling about on the sofa, obviously experiencing some discomfort, she replied,

"Yesterday, dear. I walked into town."

"Ah, right. So yesterday you were able to *Walk This Way* and that way, and so on, comfortably, without any pain?" I asked, smiling at her, then turning my head to look at Jacob's facial response. He stood looking at the floor, grinning and shaking his head, as if to say, 'that's terrible!' It was terrible, but I was clutching at straws. My mind had gone musically blank.

"Yes, yes, I was able to walk in any direction I wanted to, dear," Phyllis replied. I smiled, then continued to ask her pertinent questions regarding past medical history, prescribed medications, etcetera.

While obtaining her vital observations, I looked at her and said,

"I think you need a *Doctor, Doctor*, Phyllis." Jacob looked at me in despair. Phyllis, on the other hand, asked,

"A doctor, doctor? What's a doctor, doctor?" Before I answered her question, I glanced and smiled at Jacob.

"Two-one to me, mate."

Unhappy with me taking the lead, I could see him pondering, but it was only seconds before he came bouncing back with the equaliser.

"Phyllis, Andy meant a doctor, not a doctor-doctor. *Time After Time* Andy says the same word twice by accident," Jacob very cleverly scoring by naming Cyndi Lauper's 1983 hit.

Phyllis remained reasonably still on the sofa, so I began gently palpating her left foot, while also assessing for any obvious arthritis, bunions, general foot ailments; generally looking for a potential diagnosis.

"Phyllis, I'm pressing on your foot to assess for temperature change, pain and location of where the worst pain is, OK? *Can You Feel It?*" I asked, naming The Jacksons' 1980's hit and thinking to myself, 'three-two to me'. "Can you feel any pain when I press, at all?" I asked again, slightly altering my choice of words. Jacob once more shook his head in despair.

"Yes, yes," Phyllis replied, "it hurt more when you pressed near my big toe."

After further questioning, assessment, and asking her to walk several metres to and from the bathroom, I was happy to conclude that she needed a GP assessment. Although I didn't diagnose the condition known as gout, I was reasonably confident that was causing the pain in her left foot. After explaining that to her, I followed with,

"Don't worry, Phyllis, the GP will soon have you *Dancing On The Ceiling* again! You're not *Knockin' On Heaven's Door* just yet!"

Jacob's jaw dropped to the floor. "You sod," he said quietly. "That's five-two."

"I know, and we're nearly done here. You need to get thinking."

I continued asking Phyllis some further questions, then after some careful thinking, Jacob piped up, "Phyllis, tell me, do you drink at all?"

"Sometimes, yes. Not a lot though. Why?"

"Well, because Andy mentioned gout. Gout is known for being the disease of kings and queens, because of the sumptuously rich diet

155

and alcohol consumption of the wealthy. What do you normally drink, *Red Wine?*" Jacob asked, attempting to score a point by mentioning UB40's 1983 hit.

"Oh, only one or two glasses a day. I'm not wealthy by any measure," she replied.

"Well, if I'm right about the pain in your foot being gout," I said, "then your GP may prescribe a drug called Allopurinol, which you may have to take for the rest of your life, Phyllis. However, that's obviously for your GP to decide, not me."

Having explained my medical thoughts to her, I turned to Jacob, who was standing there with a smug grin on his face. "That's five-three, mate," he said, before I had chance to say anything. I shook my head and let out a long sigh.

"Don't look so smug, Ben. You can't have a point for red wine. The song title was *Red Red Wine*," I emphasised.

"Oh, yeah."

Phyllis still seemed absolutely oblivious to what we were referring to, which was the whole point of the challenge. I completed my documentation and contacted her GP to arrange a home visit. Jacob and I then left her at home and returned to the ambulance, where we shook hands and I was 'crowned' the winner of the eighties song title challenge.

Now both sat in the ambulance, Jacob spoke up. "We're on nights tomorrow, mate. What challenge do you suggest for tomorrow's shift?"

"Um... let me think... a-ha! Film—"

"That's a Norwegian eighties pop group, not a song title," Jacob blurted out, interrupting me.

Laughing at his retort, I said, "Film titles. Now that will be a challenge!"

Wind-Ups

Apart from playing sick and twisted pranks on each other, there was always plenty of banter amongst ambulance personnel, nurses and doctors, whether it be in the mess room of the ambulance station, parked up outside of the hospital, or inside the A&E department. The following examples are just some of the wind-ups that ambulance personnel *play* on each other.

It was common practise, upon arrival at A&E in the ambulance, to turn the engine off and place the ignition keys inside the closed sun-visor, therefore hidden from the public but readily available to the next crew member assigned to drive. It also helped to avoid misplacing the keys. Unfortunately, due to an increase in opportunistic thieves, this is no longer common practise.

Knowing full well that keys were behind the sun-visor, a typical wind-up often played on fellow crew was to drive their ambulance to another part of the hospital, so when the crew exited A&E, they'd find their vehicle was gone. This occasionally caused panic amongst 'newbies', as it wasn't condoned by management to place the keys inside the sun-visor, and more so that it had become a practise adopted by frontline ambulance personnel. Of course, the crew would eventually find their ambulance, out of sight, fifty or so yards away.

Similarly, whenever a crew admitted a patient into A&E, and the attendant had handed over their patient to the triage nurse, a crew member would then discard the used/dirty sheet, pillowcase and blanket/s, and re-cover the stretcher with fresh linen. Once complete, they would perhaps either nip to the loo, seek out the nearest vending machine, or visit the hospital shop, but on their return occasionally find their stretcher no longer where they had left it.

In some cases, it wasn't their fellow colleagues that had moved or hidden it, it was sometimes the work of an A&E nurse or doctor, as a prank on the ambulance crew. Childish? No, it was great for morale and inter-professional relationships, and both on and off-duty friendships.

Other wind-ups carried out on fellow colleagues included staff exiting the A&E department to discover that every cupboard door and drawer – and there's plenty of them – in the back of the ambulance had been opened. On occasions, the contents of the equipment cupboards and drawers had been emptied and consumables laid out neatly on the stretcher, like it had been prepared for a barrack room inspection. It was always taken in good humour and with a pinch of salt.

A simple wind-up involved folding the ambulance's wing mirrors inwards. When the driver went to move off, they would suddenly realise they couldn't effectively use the mirrors, and would have to stop and reposition them. This was many years ago, on the older type ambulances with the much smaller wing mirrors than fitted these days.

Similarly, another prank played was to move windscreen wipers away from the windscreen on a rainy day. It *usually* took the driver to sit in the cab, apply their seatbelt and start the engine, before realising they couldn't clear the screen without having to remove the seatbelt and get back out of the ambulance. It was a common act carried out in the name of humour, soon fixed and considered harmless fun.

A funny prank when an ambulance was being reversed into the station garage, mostly played on 'newbies', was to guide them back with a beckoning hand gesture, bringing them closer and closer to the back wall until the guiding crewmate would shout, "Whoa, whoa! Stop!" and then bang the palm of their hand hard on the back or side of the ambulance. It was a surprisingly convincing way to mimic the driver hitting the back wall. The driver would quickly jump out of the cab, their hand covering their mouth in shock, and then walk slowly to the back of the ambulance to inspect the damage they'd caused. The look on the driver's face was so, so funny.

Here's one of my favourite wind-ups that I played on crewmates on several separate occasions, particularly when the smaller-sized, white ambulances were in service – with wing mirrors that didn't stick out as much as my jug-ears do – not the yellow, bigger designs seen in today's modern day ambulance service. If I was still working in the NHS, I certainly wouldn't risk this following wind-up now.

While I drove us back, my crewmate would *sometimes* travel in the saloon of the ambulance in order to check what medical consumables were needed to restock the vehicle adequately for the next crew. On one particular occasion, I had been working all day alongside seasoned paramedic, Geoff. Arriving back at the station, and while Geoff was stood in the back of the ambulance checking the consumables, I noticed that the garage's ambulance parking bays were almost full of spare and operational ambulances. There was one available bay left for me to park in.

I manoeuvred the vehicle in preparedness to reverse into the garage, and Geoff kindly asked me if I wanted him to guide me back. I refused because I wanted to play a little prank on him.

As I reversed into the garage, I deliberately parked the ambulance within inches of the back wall, and as close to another parked ambulance as the nearside wing mirror would allow me to without actually banging the mirror.

As I vacated the driver's seat, Geoff attempted to open the side door from the inside, but he couldn't slide it open as there wasn't enough space between the two parked vehicles. I can only assume he then walked to the back door, looked through the glass window and realised there wasn't the space available to open it.

Meanwhile, I'd walked from the garage and into the mess room to tell the staff what I'd done. Some staff had a good old laugh, while others chose to go to the garage to see for themselves what I'd done, with me following them closely behind.

On entering the garage, we could hear Geoff shouting, "Andy, I can't get out! You've parked too close to the wall and the other ambulance!"

We were all in stitches, listening to him repeatedly shout my name while banging on the inside of the sliding door. "Andy! Andy! Are you there?! Andy!"

Then Alex shouted, "He's already left for home, and the daft sod has taken the keys with him!"

"Oh, you're joking, man! Can you ring him?!"

"I've tried to, but his phone is switched off. Just get your head down on the stretcher for the night. Andy's back on duty in the morning," James shouted.

I only left him stuck in there for several minutes before pulling the vehicle forward, allowing him to 'escape' and subsequently chase me around the garage; no harm intended, of course, just for a laugh.

Unsurprisingly, he never again remained in the saloon while driving back to the station, not when crewed with me, anyway!

Special Delivery

The following story is about me assisting in the delivery of a baby. Some paramedics go their whole career without ever being called to assist a delivery, yet I stopped counting after my 25th! I was like a magnet to women in labour.

Not all deliveries I've been involved with were in the comfort of the patient's own home. Oh no. I've attended to birthing emergencies in cars parked in lay-bys, and in the back of an ambulance while en route to the maternity ward. For safety reasons I'd always ask my driving crewmate to pull over on the roadside so I could deliver the baby while the vehicle was stationary.

The closest I got to *not* having to deliver a baby, was when my crewmate drove us to hospital on 'blues and twos' and we actually arrived on the hospital grounds, outside the entrance. However, the baby's head was crowning, and to get to the maternity ward would have meant having to use the elevator. I wasn't prepared to risk the dilemma of us getting stuck in the lift, however *highly unlikely* that was.

Neither did I think it ideal to be wheeling the patient while she was laid on the stretcher, legs akimbo, along the corridor, with onlookers witnessing the intense, traumatic ordeal she was about to endure. Therefore, I asked my crewmate to run to the ward and ask a midwife to come and help me. Despite his sprinting abilities, the baby had presented itself by the time a breathless midwife arrived.

Having given you a taster, let me explain the events of one particularly funny story that I was party to while working solo on an RRV. It was about midday and I was reading a medical book while sat on standby, waiting for an emergency to be passed to me. I responded to the dispatcher's call, "Go ahead, over."

"Roger, Andy. RED call to a thirty-two year-old in labour, waters have broken. I'll send a back-up crew when I have one, over."

"Roger. Going mobile, over."

I began driving on blue lights to the address given, and arrived outside within five minutes. I hurriedly made my way down the garden pathway, equipment in hand, including the maternity pack. I was met by the husband of the patient. He was understandably worried but appeared relieved that help had arrived.

Ascending the staircase, I could hear the woman screaming. 'A good sign,' I thought, as that meant she had not delivered the baby without having any clinical intervention from me – potentially important both before and after the baby's birth.

As I entered the bedroom, the patient was lying supine on the bed in an appropriate position to give birth, her lower body covered by a blanket. Her husband then came and stood beside her, holding her hand and offering some encouragement. I introduced myself and then learned that her name was Claire. I also learned that this would be the first time they were going to be hearing the 'pitter-patter of nappy matter' in the not too distant future.

Preparing the Entonox, I then handed it to Claire for her to self-administer. I knelt down at the end of the bed, at the 'working end', and positioned myself to crack on with the delivery. The unborn wasn't crowning, so I took the opportunity to unwrap the maternity pack and place all the equipment neatly, to keep it as close to a clinical setting as possible. I had everything I needed in the event of the best or worst-case scenario. Everything was going smoothly so far.

After I'd been on scene for several minutes, that's when the humour began to unravel. Claire's contractions had recommenced. I'm sure a lot of fathers around the globe will relate to the scene I'll now describe. At least, this is how they *might* remember it; how this uniquely wonderful and at the same time scary first-time experience is now etched in their minds.

Claire's eyes became even more wide open, her pupils becoming suddenly more dilated, and then she began clenching her teeth, grimacing, and roaring in anger. "Grrrrrrrrr!" she growled.

'Shit, what's happening?!' Her clothes and shoes suddenly became too small for her huge, bulging, muscular physique and gigantic feet. Almost everything ripped away from her body, leaving just a small, very tight-fitting pair of denim shorts in place!

'OMG, what the hell's going on?!' Her skin colour appeared to change from white to a dark pea green colour. Her hair looked like it hadn't seen a hairbrush in years, nor had her eyebrows ever been trimmed! She looked as if she could grab the heaviest thing, even her hubby, pick him up above her head and throw him across the bedroom. As much as the paramedic tried to help, she went to grab his arm and I imagined her throwing me through the glass of the bedroom window, from where I'd fall two floors to my death!

Yes... you guessed it... she had transformed into the Incredible Hulk!

And wake up... you're back in the room, back in the room.

"You!" she said, turning to face her hubby with a scary, aggressive facial expression. "You are going nowhere near me again, you b*****d!"

"Calm down, love, calm down. I'm here, don't worry," he replied, his hand being crushed by her grasp.

"Don't you tell me to calm down, you stupid shit! I hate you for doing this to me! Arrrrrrrrrrrrgh! Arrrrrrrrrrrrrrrrrgh!" she screamed through gritted teeth.

I continued encouraging Claire to push when it was the right time to do so, and also made mental notes of how many minutes passed between contractions.

"Arrrrrrrrrrrrgh!" she screamed as the second bout began.

"Push, love. Push! You're doing well, sweetie," hubby said, quite calmly.

Once again, through clenched teeth she responded with, "Don't you tell me when to push, you b*****d! Arrrrrrrrrrrgh! You're sleeping on the sofa for the rest of your life, you useless piece of shit!"

Still situated at the 'working end', gloved up and ready to catch the slippery future rug-rat, I had to subtly grin to myself. I'd often heard similar expletives of hatred and anger aimed at the onlooking, doting father-to-be, while they were doing their utmost best to support their wife or partner.

The contractions ceased once more, and still no crowning was evident. Still no arrival of a back-up ambulance crew either. But while I continued to offer words of encouragement to Claire, ambulance control contacted me. "Go ahead, over."

"Roger. There should be a crew with you in about five minutes. Is everything going OK there? Over."

"Roger. Many thanks. Yeah, going smooth so far. Patient still in labour, over," I replied, but thinking, 'well, smooth for me, but not for the Hulk and her hubby'.

Claire's contractions started again. "Arrrrrrrrrrrrrrrrrrrrrrrrrrrgh!" she screamed. "I f***in' hate you!"

I almost expected her head to do a 360 degree turn and then for her to projectile vomit and start hurling Satan-like abuse, like a scene from *The Exorcist*. In reality I was still holding back my laughter, and patiently waiting for the baby's head to begin crowning.

A few more minutes went by and the back-up crew arrived. I could hear them walking up the stairs, but just as the crew entered the bedroom, Claire screamed again and shouted, "Get that shit who's done this to me out of here now!"

Consequently, Don replied, "Sorry, love, but not guilty. I've never met you before in my life." My head dropped and I burst out laughing.

"Not you! Him!" she shouted, referring to her husband, before letting out another scream.

The baby's head began crowning, so my laughter ceased with the seriousness of the situation.

"Push Claire, push," I said calmly. My back-up crew were there for support and so stood by, ready for any intervention that might be needed once the baby had fully presented itself to the big, wide world.

Claire screamed out again, staring at her hubby with raging eyes. "You f**king useless, lanky streak of piss, pack your f**kin' bags now!"

With a grin on his face, Don looked at him and said, "Bloody hell, mate, what have you done to her?"

"Got her up the duff, 'aven't I, but I won't be doing it again, I'll tell you that!" he replied. "I've never gotten so much abuse."

"F**k off you d**khead. You're gettin' the snip, you shit!"

"I thought you said I couldn't go anywhere near you again, so why would I need to get the snip?" he asked. Myself and Don burst out laughing at his comeback and I thought, 'Oh dear,' but instead said,

"She's going to give you a vasectomy herself, mate. I can see it."

"I'm f**kin' gonna chop it off altogether, and sew it to your head, you d**khead!" she said through gritted teeth. Once again, with the exception of Claire, the room filled with laughter.

After several more minutes of screaming abuse at her hubby, further contractions, and Claire pushing, a little baby boy presented himself to the world.

After catching the slippery little fella in my hands, I noted the time of birth, quickly dried him down and handed him to his relieved mum. As Claire and her hubby adored their new son, I carried out an APGAR score, which was adequate and satisfactory.

I carefully counted his tiny fingers and toes to ensure the correct number and, with tongue in cheek, checked that they weren't webbed! Then I ruffled through his dark brown hair to make sure he didn't have *666* on his scalp. No, I didn't do that... I may have *thought* of doing it. I then had to wait for the placenta to emerge, and also for a midwife to arrive and decide whether Claire and the future rug-rat needed to be taken to hospital or not.

Overall, everything had gone smoothly, and Claire was by now calm and, while lying on the bed, gave her hubby and their newborn a loving kiss and cuddle following the traumatic ordeal. Altogether now... Aww.

Sheer Ignorance

Prior to the implementation of the NHS 111 service, part of my role as an NHS paramedic was to man the telephone triage desk for the GP Out-of-Hours service (OoH). This service was available on weekdays, after the GP surgeries had closed, and twenty-four hours a day on Saturday and Sunday.

The role involved sitting at a desk equipped with a keyboard, two monitors and a telephone with headset, though I wouldn't always use the headset. There, I'd wait for a call taker to ascertain a caller's details and input them onto the system before passing the information on to me via the computer system. I would then open the incident detail and call the patient back, or whoever had called on behalf of the patient.

Upon them answering, I'd introduce myself as a paramedic and thoroughly question them to determine the patient's presenting signs and symptoms, in addition to any other significant history. I'd then offer either self-care advice, arrange a GP to visit them in their home – depending on their age, mobility, etcetera – or ask them to attend the clinic at a specific time. On rare occasions I'd dispatch an emergency ambulance to them.

I have to be honest, I hated it. I much preferred to assess patients face to face, physically observing the patient's clinical presentation myself. Via the telephone, you could only rely on the information given by the caller, and their perceived seriousness of the symptoms they were complaining of. But while it wasn't a role I enjoyed, there were occasional calls that had me and my fellow telephonists cracked up with laughter.

Case in point: this next incident occurred at about 6am one sunny Sunday morning. I'd been on duty, manning the GP out-of-hours service desk, since 7pm the previous evening, and had dealt with more than fifty calls throughout the night. I was exhausted and just wanted to go home and inspect the insides of my eyelids.

I was very close to the end of my shift when an incident popped up on the monitor, which displayed: **Name:** Pearl. **Age:** 70. **Clinical Concern:** Abdominal Pain.

Deciding not to bother wearing the headset, as my jug-ears were hurting from wearing it all night, I decided to simply pick up the telephone receiver instead, and dialled the patient's contact number. After several rings, the phone was answered.

"Hello."

"Hello, is that Pearl?" I asked.

"No, it's her friend and neighbour," the lady replied. From her very posh, snobbish tone of voice, I could have sworn I was speaking to Hyacinth Bucket (pronounced Bouquet), from the BBC sitcom, '*Keeping Up Appearances*'.

"Oh, right. Well, my name's Andy. I'm a paramedic calling from the GP out-of-hours service. Could I ask who I'm speaking to, please?"

"My name is Constance," she replied. "I will be speaking on behalf of Pearl, thank you very much."

'Rude and stern' came to mind!

"OK, Constance, that's fine, but you will need to keep repeating the questions that I want to ask Pearl regarding her abdominal pain. Then you will need to relay her answers to me. Is there no chance she could come to the phone and speak to me directly?" I politely asked.

"No, she's in pain and unable to speak for herself. As I said, I will be speaking on her behalf."

Initially, I began to think that this was going to be a very tiring, end-of-nightshift, patient telephone assessment... I was wrong. It actually turned out to be a very funny experience!

I began my clinical questioning through the third-party caller, Hyacinth... that is, Constance. The following conversation with 'Hyacinth' not only surprised *me* a little, but also astonished the duty GPs, and my fellow triage clinician, too. The call had them laughing hysterically in the background, whereas I had to somehow hold my laughter in. 'Hyacinth's' sheer ignorance was hilarious!

The first conversation went something like this:

Me: "Can you ask Pearl what time the pain came on, please?"

Hyacinth: "It came on about three hours ago."

Me: "You didn't ask her. You've answered for her. Can you ask her, please?"

Hyacinth: "No, I won't. She told me the pain came on at two this morning."

Me: "Well it's gone six now, so that's more like four hours."

Hyacinth: "Don't be cantankerous, you pugnacious, silly man! I rang the out-of-hours to speak to a doctor and tell them to visit Pearl. Stop this silly questioning, and send a doctor at once!"

Following 'Hyacinth's' comment, I decided to activate the loudspeaker button so it could be heard by all those in the out-of-hours hub.

Me: "Excuse me, this is not silly questioning. This is pertinent clinical questioning that needs to be asked in order for me to reach a decision on the most appropriate healthcare professional required for Pearl, whether that be a GP, a paramedic or, as a paramedic, self-care advice from myself."

Hyacinth: "She needs a doctor, not self-care advice, and certainly

172

not from an ambulance driver or first-aider!"

I could hear laughter coming from behind me in the out-of-hours hub.

Me: "I didn't say an ambulance driver, I said a paramedic."

Hyacinth: "Same difference. What's a paramedic going to do? Just send a doctor to the house at once!"

Me: "I'm sorry, but a paramedic is a highly trained, registered healthcare professional, they don't simply drive an ambulance."

Hyacinth: "Of course they do. What else could a paramedic possibly do other than drive a patient to hospital to see a doctor? Send a doctor to Pearl immediately. I insist!"

I could hear more laughter from the GPs and my fellow triage clinician in the background.

Me: "That's not how the GP out-of-hours service works, I'm afraid. Now, if you allow me to ask you further questions to repeat to Pearl, and you relay her answers back to me, then I'll be able to arrange the most appropriate healthcare professional for her or, alternatively, offer self-care advice."

Hyacinth: "This is a complete waste of time being questioned by an ambulance driver."

Me: "You've misunderstood. After I have assessed Pearl via the telephone, as a qualified, experienced, professionally registered paramedic, I will triage Pearl and reach a decision on the most appropriate clinician to visit her at home, if necessary. It may be a doctor, a paramedic or an ECP."

Hyacinth: "What's an ECP?"

Me: "To keep it simple, an ECP is a paramedic with additional training, knowledge and skills."

Hyacinth: "Oh, really? An advanced ambulance driver, you mean?"

By now I was holding my hand over my mouth to stop me from laughing down the telephone line.

Me: "Look, it'd be much easier if I speak to Pearl directly. You're wasting time and delaying me from reaching a clinical impression of the cause of her abdominal pain, and therefore from arranging a timely response from the most appropriate healthcare professional."

Hyacinth: "Oh, forget it. I'm not being patronised by a first-aid driver. Goodbye!" 'Hyacinth' slammed the phone down.

I couldn't believe it. She was so ignorant that she put Pearl's health and safety at risk. My colleague, and the doctors, fully aware of what 'Hyacinth' had been saying, were laughing and chuckling nearby. I decided to take a few moments to release *my* laughter, too.

After one doctor had composed herself, she offered to ring 'Hyacinth' back, to save me further insult and frustration, but I insisted on seeing the call through. And anyway, I wasn't insulted, I thought it was hilarious and a great call to end my shift with.

I returned to my desk and redialled Pearl's home phone number. After several rings, the phone was answered for a second time. The follow-up conversation went something like this:

Me: "Hello, it's Andy from the GP out-of-hours service. Is that—?"

Hyacinth: "Oh, you again! I was hoping it was a doctor ringing. What do you want?!"

Me: "You slammed the phone down on me. I don't appreciate that at all. Pearl is my patient, not you. Please do not put the phone down on me again."

Hyacinth: "I didn't put the phone down on you. You must have hung up on me."

Me: "No, I didn't, but it doesn't matter. Pearl's health is what matters. Now, are you going to allow me to ask further questions, or can you put Pearl on the phone, please?"

Hyacinth: "Continue with your silly questions then, ask away if you think you're qualified enough to."

Me: "Believe me, I am. Now, can you ask Pearl where the pain in her abdomen is, as in upper and/or lower, left and/or right side, please?"

I could hear 'Hyacinth' relaying the question to Pearl. Moments later, the conversation continued.

Hyacinth: "Hello. She said it's in the lower part of her stomach."

Me: "OK. Can you ask her if she's been urinating and passing bowel movements normally, please?"

Hyacinth: "I certainly will not, young man! That's very personal!"

Me: "Yes, I appreciate they're personal, intrusive questions, but they're important questions which a doctor would ask Pearl. That's why it'd be much more appropriate if I spoke to Pearl directly."

Hyacinth: "Well, she can't come to the phone. She's in too much pain."

Me: "Right. Can you ask her, on a scale of zero to ten, what she would score the pain as, please?"

Hyacinth: "It's about a three."

Me: "You didn't ask her."

Hyacinth: "Well from her grimace, it looks like a three."

Me: "You can't judge somebody else's pain score, Hyacinth."

Hyacinth: "Hyacinth? My name is Constance."

Me: "Sorry, my mistake."

'Hyacinth' then relayed the question to Pearl.

The GPs were still nearby, listening in to the conversation, evidently still finding it funny judging by the audible signs of their amusement that I could hear. I, however, was becoming frustrated from not being able to speak with Pearl directly. I wanted to be able to ask a lot more questions, much quicker.

Hyacinth: "She says it's a four out of ten. What's that got to do with anything? Just send a doctor will you, for heaven's sake."

Me: "Sorry, but this isn't helping Pearl, it's only delaying help. What I'm going to do is arrange an ECP to visit Pearl at home. The ECP will be about twenty to thirty minutes or so, OK?"

Hyacinth: "What's he going to do, he's not a doctor?"

Me: "No, she! *She* is not a doctor. Nevertheless, she's a registered healthcare professional who will fully assess and examine Pearl at home and decide if she needs to go to hospital or not. She will also undertake an ECG, with an ECG machine which the out-of-hours GP doesn't carry with them. Is that OK?"

Hyacinth: "Well, if an ECP is all you've got, then I suppose it will have to do."

Following that comment, I couldn't hold in my laughter any longer. I laughed out loud. The doctors were open-mouthed, horrified by such an ignorant comment from 'Hyacinth'. Hearing my laughter, the conversation continued.

Hyacinth: "What are you laughing at? I do hope you are not laughing at me, young man?!"

Me: "No, no. I'm laughing at something I've just seen through the window, that's all."

Hyacinth: "What was it?"

Me: 'Nosey cow. What's it got to do with you?' I thought. "It's irrelevant. Now, the ECP is on her way, so I'm going to hang up now, Mrs Buck— Constance. OK?"

Expecting her to slam the phone down again, I didn't wait for a response. I placed the telephone handset down and let out a big sigh of relief, then had another chuckle with the GPs and my fellow clinician.

I had been due to finish at 7am, but I got delayed with another out-of-hours incident, causing me to finish late. However, it was fortunate in a way because Shelley, the ECP, came to see me in the clinical hub after attending to Pearl. Her face was a picture when she said to me,

"What the hell did you just send me to, Andy?"

"Why, what was the problem? I take it you met the lovely Hyacinth?"

"Who?"

"Sorry, I meant Constance."

Furrowing her eyebrows, Shelley replied, "Lovely?! She was an absolute nightmare. She spoke to me like I was something she'd scraped off her shoe! Pearl was lovely, she appeared embarrassed by her friend's brash, ignorant behaviour towards me. She was no trouble."

Laughing, I replied, "Well, her friend doesn't think much of us mere 'ambulance drivers', or even you advanced 'ambulance drivers'." Shelley looked at me with an expression of disgust.

"Eh, is that what she said?"

"Yep. What was the outcome, anyway?"

"Well, I did a full examination including a twelve-lead ECG. All of her vitals were normal. I put it down to mild constipation, gave self-care advice, and left her at home," she said.

Hearing that I had to laugh, because 'Hyacinth' had made such a fuss about wanting a doctor, when a home visit from an ECP proved more than adequate for Pearl.

Red-Faced

It's common, where possible and due to the nature of the job, to have mixed-sex ambulance personnel working together. It can prove beneficial for many reasons, but in particular to prevent embarrassment for patients. Some calls involve intrusive examinations on both male and female patients, young, middle-aged or elderly.

In this next incident, my good friend and paramedic crewmate, Izzie, was sat in the attendant's seat. I was driving when we were contacted by the dispatcher, one midweek afternoon. "Go ahead, over."

"Roger, Izzie. RED call to an eighteen-year-old male complaining of profuse bleeding from his penis, over."

"Do we know the cause, over?" Izzie asked, as it was an uncommon type of incident to be called to.

"No, his girlfriend, the caller, gave very little detail, over."

En route I said, with a slight wincing expression on my face, and sucking air in through my clenched teeth, "He's probably caught his winky in his zipper. That scene from 'Something about Mary' springs to mind."

"Oh no, and I'm attending. You might have to deal with this one," Izzie said.

Arriving at the property, we wandered inside to find a teenaged girl sat on the sofa, and the young man, our patient, fully clothed, pacing about with both of his hands cupped around his 'private region'.

Izzie introduced us to them both and then began questioning him while he still paced the room, evidently in some distress. There were signs of claret on his tracksuit bottoms, and a little on his hands.

"What's your name, love?" Izzie asked.

"Paul," he answered, still pacing.

"OK Paul, what's happened then?" He stopped pacing the lounge and sat down on the sofa, but remained fidgety, still cupping his hands around his prized possession.

"I went for a wee and caught my, erm... you know what... in my fly. There's a lot of blood," he explained. I winced again as I knew how he felt. I've done it once only in my entire life, but I know it does a lot more than just tickle.

Izzie looked at me and asked, "What should I do? Do I need to look, or do you want to look instead?"

"Oh, you don't have to look, do you? Can we not just go to hospital?" he asked. By this point his cheeks appeared flushed, through pain, embarrassment or both. Izzie turned to me once more for an answer.

"You're perfectly entitled to refuse examination, and I'd understand. However, you may need a dressing putting on to stop the bleeding," I explained. "It's your call. There's nothing to be embarrassed about, though. Izzie can look away if that makes you feel any better?"

"OK," he replied, "as long as she turns away."

Izzie turned her back and the lad dropped his tracksuit bottoms and his underwear to his ankles. On inspection, there was no profuse bleeding, but straightaway I could see what he'd done. I pondered for a moment, sceptical about what he'd said had caused his penile injury. I removed a small dressing from the parabag, unwrapped it and asked him to place it into his underwear and pull his trackies back up.

After doing so, he sat down on the sofa, still cupping his injured 'little fella', and I informed Izzie that she could turn back around. His girlfriend remained sat on the sofa, mute, though slightly red-faced, too.

"What's the score, Andy?" Izzie asked.

"Um, one-nil to nature," I replied.

"Eh?"

"I'm not convinced he's tellin' us the truth," I said to Izzie out loud, with an obvious display of doubt on my face. "Are you tellin' me the truth, Paul?"

Rocking back and forth on the sofa, he said, "Yeah, why?"

Looking down at the floor and shaking my head, I replied, "Because if you catch your willy in your zipper, you have to unzip back down to release the 'skin' from the zip. Your injury doesn't suggest that's what's happened at all," I said with a cringingly graphic explanation of the mechanism of the alleged, embarrassing injury.

"What are you thinking then?" Izzie asked. I glanced at Izzie, then turned back to Paul.

"You've torn your frenulum and—"

"My what?!" he asked.

"Your frenulum... your 'banjo string', pal. That's not likely to occur catching your John-Thomas in your zipper," I said. "Now, why don't you just tell me the truth, because I've got a good idea what's happened here today anyway, buddy."

"I don't know what you mean," he replied, now becoming a little more flushed. Izzie stood mute, probably through curiosity as I don't think she'd grasped what I was implying. Paul's girlfriend, on the other hand, appeared a little bashful, sheepish and, I sensed, mortified at the situation as she remained quietly sat on the sofa next to Paul.

"Is this your address or your girlfriend's?" I asked.

"It's my address," the girl said, speaking for the first time since we'd arrived.

"Where are your parents then, love? At work?"

"Yeah, until about six o'clock."

"And are you over sixteen?" I asked with significance.

"Yeah, I'm eighteen," she answered.

I was treading carefully. I didn't want to embarrass them both, but I had to come clean with what I was thinking, and was just about to when Paul's girlfriend stood up from the sofa and walked into the adjoining kitchen. It was then Izzie and I spotted something that would potentially confirm my cause of injury... there was a fresh, red blood stain near the backside area of her white, Lycra leggings.

"OK, I'm going to be frank with you both... as opposed to being Andy," I said to add a little lightheartedness to the atmosphere, and hopefully put Paul a little more at ease, ready for what I was about to say. "When she comes back in from the kitchen. OK?"

Moments later, Paul's girlfriend returned to the lounge and sat back down next to Paul. Alternating my gaze back and forth between the two of them, I said,

"Don't be embarrassed. Now, are you happy to hear my thoughts about the cause of your injury, Paul?" Both he and his girlfriend nodded their approval. "I think you've been sexually experimenting with anal sex." I glanced at the young lady, "Are you aware that you have blood coming from your backside? It's all over the back of your leggings." Izzie covered her mouth with her hand to prevent a giggle. "And Paul, you've torn your 'banjo string', it's hanging off. Have you had unprotected anal sex?"

182

Paul and his girlfriend's faces lit up like warning signs on an instrument panel, causing Paul to remove his hands from cupping below, to placing his palms over his face in embarrassment. They didn't need to answer my question, it was obvious from their body language.

"I don't want to lecture you both, but if you're gonna do it up the 'bum-holey', 'poo-chute', or whatever it is you youngsters call it these days, then I suggest you use a condom and some lube," I advised them, not mincing my words. Izzie stood close by, still holding her hand over her mouth, her stomach almost vibrating as if she wanted to burst out laughing at my choice of words.

"We just thought we'd try it, mate. I won't be doin' it again, I tell you that!" he emphasised. "Do I have to go to hospital?"

"Well... a torn 'banjo string' can heal itself. Then again, surgery is sometimes necessary. I'd strongly advise that you seek further medical advice at the minor injury clinic, plus you should both be tested for STDs." They both looked at me with horror on their faces. Izzie stood there grinning.

"Will our parents have to be told?" Paul asked with a fearful expression.

"No. You're both eighteen, so you have the privilege of patient confidentiality. I'll complete the paperwork and leave a copy with you to hand in to the nurse." I turned to Paul's girlfriend, "I'd go and change your clothes before you go to the clinic." Then back to Paul, "Can I trust you to follow my advice about going to the minor injury clinic? Can you make your own way there, or do you want us to take you in the ambulance?"

"I'll drive there when you've finished here," Paul replied.

After thoroughly completing the non-conveyance form and handing Paul a carbon-copy to take to hospital with him, Izzie and I vacated the property and returned to the ambulance. There in the cab, Izzie let out a huge belly laugh, and as I moved off from the roadside, she asked, "How did you not laugh in there?"

"Sympathy! The poor bugger... no pun intended!" I replied.

"What do you mean, *you've* experienced tearing your 'banjo' doin' anal?" she asked. Turning to her with a puzzled expression, I replied,

"No, that'd be empathy. I sympathise with him because I can only imagine the panic he was feeling, having never experienced tearing my 'banjo string'."

The above is not an isolated case of a torn 'banjo string' that I've had to attend to during my career. I attended to a sixteen-year-old lad who had decided to experiment with his girlfriend while his parents were away on holiday, and did the same thing as Paul and his girlfriend.

More shockingly, I attended an incident where a sixty-six-year-old pensioner had no reservations whatsoever in informing me that he'd had his 'banjo string' torn by his girlfriend who was thirty years his junior. And then went on to inform me that it was while she was, um... uh-hmm... mast... uh-hmm... masturbating him. Ugh!

Stand-Off

I chose to write this story in honour of my late friend and former colleague, Sonia (a.k.a. Sonic). She was a fantastic paramedic, great fun to work with, and possessed a wicked sense of humour... like *most* frontline ambulance personnel!

Sonia and I were crewed together, one cold December night, and were at the start of a twelve-hour nightshift. At approximately 6:05pm, a RED call was passed to us via my handheld radio. "Go ahead, over," I said to the dispatcher.

"Roger, RED call for you. You're responding to a thirty-year-old male holding a kitchen knife, over."

"Roger. Can you elaborate, please? I'm sure there's thousands of people up and down the country holding a kitchen knife; it's just gone six o'clock, over." There was humour in my tone and Sonia began laughing. She had an animated smile and infectious laugh to match, so it set me off, too.

"Yeah, sorry. He's brandishing a knife in the kitchen, and possibly a machete! His partner and children are inside the house, too. Stand-off, though. I repeat, stand-off until armed response arrive, over."

"Roger, going mobile, over," I replied, as Sonia switched on the 'blues and twos' and headed to the address given.

We arrived, but as per procedure, Sonia parked up out of sight, rather than outside the address – best not to be seen by someone suspected of wielding a knife and machete if he peers through a window!

I informed ambulance control that we were on scene but were standing-off nearby. There was still no sign of an armed police unit, so we sat in the cab, with the heating on, and waited... and waited...

And waited. After twenty or so minutes of chatting together, I turned to Sonia and said, "Where the hell are the police? This is ridiculous, he could have stabbed them all by now." I thought for a moment. "I've got an idea, Sonia."

"Go on," she said, looking intrigued.

"I think we should go in anyway. Sod waiting for the police."

"No chance!"

"Wait, wait. Hear me out," I said. "I think we should go in, then while I confront him and attempt to calm the situation, you discreetly kneel down and tie his shoe laces together." Sonia gave me an old-fashioned smile, as if to say 'are you serious?' "Then you... again very discreetly, get on all fours behind him and I'll push him over you. It's foolproof. It can't possibly go wrong!"

Sonia, with her animated smile, burst out laughing, causing me to howl with laughter too. Then, composing herself, she asked, "What if he's not wearing any shoes?"

"Good point. OK, let's go to plan 'B'," I said, looking serious. "We go in, and again while I'm trying to calm the situation, I'll suddenly tug both of his ears, while you tickle him until he can't take any more." Just visualising such a scenario had us both laughing out loud some more.

"What if he's not ticklish?" Sonia asked, still smiling.

"Good point. OK, let's go to plan 'C'," I said. "We tie a long piece of string to an aluminium bottle top and place it into the letterbox. Then, we unravel the string and move away a good distance from the property. We then pull the string, which will cause the bottle top to flap the letterbox. When he comes outside to see if anybody's there, we run and leg it into the house and lock him out."

By now, tears of laughter were rolling down Sonia's face. "What if he doesn't step out of the house to see if anybody's there?"

187

"Good point. Let's go to plan 'D' then."

"Which is?" she asked, with that beaming smile on her face.

"Plan 'D' is this... this one's foolproof, trust me. While we're waiting for the police, we nip to the local Indian takeaway, order some onion bhajis, poppadums, two lamb bhunas, some pilau rice and a naan bread, then we'll pretend to be a delivery service. As he opens the front door, you throw a lamb bhuna in his face and I'll disarm and restrain him. As I'm doing that, you crack some poppadums over his face, and stuff his mouth with broken pieces. Simple! What could possibly go wrong?"

Sonia's eyes once again began to stream with tears of laughter rolling down her face. Trying to compose herself, she asked, "What if the police arrive while we're in the takeaway?"

"Good point. Let's discuss plan 'H' then."

"'H'... what happened to plan 'E'?"

"Look, Sonia," I said sternly, "I've put a lot of thought into plans 'E', 'F' and 'G', but they're all silly and simply won't work like my previous plans would've done. Plan 'E', 'F' and 'G' were too farfetched, unrealistic and were, quite frankly, ridiculous!"

By now, Sonia was crossing her legs and howling with laughter. "I'm gonna wet myself, Andy!"

We'd been on scene for about half an hour by now and there was still no sign of an armed response unit; so I continued explaining my ridiculous plan of action.

"Plan 'H', Sonia, is this," I said, with a very serious facial expression. "You drive up to the property, park up in obvious view of the assailant's house. Meanwhile, I'll discreetly shimmy up the drainpipe and climb onto the roof. You then knock on the front door and tell him you're a Morrisons delivery driver; you'll look convincing, trust me, with the ambulance parked outside his house. Tell the machete-wielding maniac that you have his shopping. As you say that, I'll abseil from the roof and smash through the bedroom window and rescue his partner and kids. It's foolproof, hun. What could possibly go wrong?!"

"A lot, Andy," Sonia replied, laughing.

I mentioned, obviously in humour, the Morrisons delivery van, because it is absolutely true. If you're reading this and are a former or present employee of the frontline NHS Ambulance Service, then you'll know only too well that a Morrisons delivery van looks like an ambulance, particularly while driving along on a dark night. There's probably not one frontline ambulance man or woman up and down the country that hasn't given a gestural flash of their headlights to an oncoming Morrisons delivery van driver, particularly while driving in the dark, mistaking the van for a fellow colleague. I did it countless times during the first several hours of a twelve-hour nightshift, more so during the autumn and winter seasons.

Back to the story. A short time later, the armed police arrived on scene and we accompanied them inside the property. There we found a man, his partner and two children. The man wasn't in possession of a machete or a kitchen knife, and none of them had sustained any injuries. As no ambulance was required, Sonia and I vacated the property, leaving the police to deal with the situation.

Sonia and I cleared with ambulance control and were immediately passed another RED call which, incidentally, turned out to involve even more painful belly laughing!

Paintball Fun

From time to time, a fellow colleague or I would organise an inter-station fun day or night out: Ten-Pin bowling, Go-Kart racing, a night of frivolity on the nightclub strip, or some other event. This next incident is centred around a day out partaking in the painful, extreme sport of 'paintballing'.

After a lot of organising over several weeks, a number of ambulance personnel from several stations rendezvoused at the paintballing location. Members of the public, and other emergency service personnel, were present, too.

All participants were congregated together, sat on benches in the three-sided 'safe-shed'. Some, including myself, donned full khaki camouflaged attire. As an ice-breaker, we all briefly explained where we were from and where we worked, etcetera. There was approximately thirty or forty people of mixed sexes present, including some off-duty police officers from the armed response unit.

Also amongst the group, sat opposite me, was a young man in his twenties. He evidently had the condition called Tourette's. I wasn't alone in noticing that he frequently blurted out random words. I do feel sorry for people with Tourette's, but hearing random tics does tickle my sense of humour.

The chap, Conner, announced to the group that he had Tourette's, and explained that he would not be offended should anyone find his tics funny. He informed us that he too found his random tics funny. Fortunately, that put the group at ease. My first thought was, 'This should be interesting. How on earth is he going to avoid giving his position up?'

Following a safety briefing, and purchasing some paintballs to place into the weapon's hopper, one of the safety marshals began to explain what the outline of the first game was going to involve.

"OK. For the first game, you're going to be paired up," he shouted, needlessly as we were only a few feet away from him. I'm sure he must have been an ex-army drill sergeant or something similar, because everything he said, he shouted.

The marshal appointed each individual 'trooper' (participant) as either a trooper in team 'A' or a trooper in team 'B'. Another marshal handed out black safety helmets to those in team 'A', and green helmets to those in team 'B'. Each trooper was paired up with somebody from their team. I was paired with Conner, in team 'A'.

He seemed like a nice bloke, after having a quick chat with him prior to the first game starting. He did occasionally blurt out some random words which – I'm not going to lie – did cause me to laugh, but he didn't mind, and he laughed at himself. But his Tourette's would potentially prove detrimental to our 'survival' as a pair while trying to complete the object of the mission. It would likely also determine how quickly we'd both be sat back in the safe-shed, waiting for the game to finish; if you're hit with a paintball, you're out of the game – classed as K.I.A (killed in action).

"OK. Let the game commence!" one of the several safety marshals shouted. Each team quickly departed from the safe-shed and took up a chosen position in the dense woodland. Team 'A' coupled themselves in their appointed pairs and spread out at one end of the woods. Team 'B' located themselves at the opposite end.

We were given five minutes to prepare for battle. Some of us chose to temporarily remove our safety goggles and rub soil on our faces, and place foliage into our safety helmets and clothing. For those of you who know the game, I like sniping when I go paintballing, but, being paired with Conner, I decided not to snipe during the first game.

The marshal blew his whistle loudly, informing all troops that the game had started. Conner and I, now suitably camouflaged, began stealthily moving through the woods in the prone position. After a couple of minutes, we could hear the sound of compressed gas as paintballs were being fired. Communicating with Conner, I said, "Right, keep low, move quietly and stay within the heavily wooded areas."

"OK, bud," he replied.

We quietly began moving through the long grass and fern, using large trees as cover, ready for action. I heard several enemy troops approaching our position. As the enemy got closer and closer to us, all of a sudden Conner shouted,

"We're over here! Tea leaf! Chicken feed!"

I couldn't help but burst into laughter. If Conner hadn't already compromised us, I certainly had by the volume of my laughter. Laughing at his own tics, Conner said, "I'm sorry, mate... biscuits! Rich tea! My tics come on when I'm excited or anxious."

I was still laughing as he shouted, "We're here, scruffy!"

Continuing to giggle, I asked him, "Well, what are you now, excited or anxious?"

"Both," he replied. "Chicken feed!" Then paintballs began whizzing past us, hitting nearby trees and bushes.

Conner and I quickly stood and ran, repositioning ourselves behind a different tree. The enemy, however, gave slow chase and saw where we were hiding. They shot several paintballs in our direction, missing us both by inches. Knelt up, I popped my head from around the bush and fired several paintballs, hitting two enemy troops in the chest, taking them both out of the game. Two more were still nearby, though, so Conner and I quietly retreated further back, away from them.

Having found a safe hiding place, Conner tapped me on the shoulder. "OK, I've got an idea. You go left flank, quietly and...

Quavers... multipack," he said. Well, I just couldn't contain my loud laughter yet again. Conner began to laugh too, contributing to compromising our position. "Qua... Qua... Quavers! You go left flank, quietly, and work your way round and approach them from behind. We can use my tics to our advantage."

"In what respect?" I asked.

"Chick... chicken feed. Rich tea. Two, please!" he blurted out. I was crouched, but his tic caused me to collapse to the ground with laughter, and have to wipe tears from my eyes before I could continue listening to his plan. "When you're in position, I'll shout something to compromise myself... Quavers... then when they find me... tea bag... you take them out, preferably before they shoot me," he explained. I cracked up, laughing uncontrollably once again, and I could barely concentrate on observing for the slowly approaching enemy. "Qua... Quavers."

"OK," I said, "good plan."

So off I went, quietly manoeuvring left flank through the woods. I could hear the compressed air as paintballs were being shot around the woodlands. As I stealthily flanked around the two troops, and had them in my sights, I could see them approach Conner.

"I'm over here, scruffy hair! Quavers!" he shouted as he emerged from a bush. I heard the two enemy troops laughing while simultaneously aiming their weapons at Conner. I pulled the trigger and splatted both of them with several paintballs.

After a further ten minutes of battle, with Conner and I still unscathed, the marshal blew his whistle; all of Team 'B' had been K.I.A. First game over.

As all the participants, most of them covered in paint, sat down in the safe-shed, the marshal explained game two.

"OK, this time you're still in teams, but you're not paired up. You're individually in Team 'A' and Team 'B'," he announced loudly. "If you were in Team 'A' last time, you're now Team 'B', and vice-versa." Several of us immediately frowned in confusion, but it was Conner who spoke up.

"That doesn't make sense, chief... Quavers. Team 'A' or 'B', we've still got the same people on our team... paint... paintball... robin red breast, over there," he said.

Myself, my station colleagues, and several of those that I didn't know, none of us could help but burst into laughter. He was right, there was a robin red breast sat on a branch of a nearby tree. Conner again wasn't at all fazed by us laughing, he too laughed at himself. The marshal wasn't laughing, though.

"Oh yeah, good point," he replied. "OK, half of Team 'A' now join Team 'B' and vice-versa, and half of each team swap your colour helmets. You decide. Quickly, quickly! Let's go!" he ordered with bellowing assertion.

The marshal then explained the object of the second game; it was a straightforward team battle within the surroundings of the woodlands. Conner was now on the opposite team.

As the teams parted once again and we individually positioned ourselves at opposite sides of the woods, I reapplied some soil to my face and lay in a prone position in a huge bush. There, I patiently waited in a sniping position for some of the enemy to approach.

A few minutes went by, and I could hear shots being fired and audible frustrations echoing around the woods from people being shot and taken out of the game within minutes of the start. As I lay sniping, I heard two people approaching my position... one of them was Conner!

"We're coming! Chick... chicken feed!" Conner shouted. The other trooper, walking just several feet away from him, whispered,

"Shush. I'm counting on you to control your tics, mate."

"Counting down... Rachel Riley! Sorry, mate," he loudly replied.

"That's Countdown, not counting down," I heard Conner's teammate reply.

Spotting them both approaching, about fifteen feet from the bush that I was laid in, I took my moment and let off a single paintball straight at the chest of Conner. *SPLAT*. His mate dropped to his knees and attempted to take some cover. I thought the sound of the compressed gas from my weapon would expose my position, but it didn't.

"Snipe... sniper. Where did that... Quavers... come from?!" Conner asked his teammate. Seconds later, I shot a single paintball and hit the other trooper's safety goggles.

A nearby safety marshal sent them packing and they both headed back to the safe-shed, Conner shouting, "Chicken feed! We're dead! Shaggy hair!" as he ambled through the woods, still unaware of where I was hiding. I had to clamp my teeth onto my finger to resist the urge to laugh out loud at his vocal tics. I could hear other enemy troops' footsteps approaching nearby. As two of them got closer, I let off a barrage of paintballs, taking both out of the game.

Having plenty of paintballs still in my weapon's hopper, I emerged from the bush and stealthily crept through the woodland to seek out some more action. Taking cover behind stacked wooden pallets and empty, rusty oil barrels, I spotted one of the off-duty armed coppers stood in a deep, dug-out trench. Assuming he was going to be a 'good shot', I made my way carefully and quietly through the foliage.

Shooting, shouting and echoes of pain from being shot, resonated around the woods. I could clearly see troops wandering back towards the safe-shed, their clothes covered in paint and, therefore, out of the game. I wanted a challenge; to survive an assault on the armed copper would be great fun.

I spent several minutes in the prone position, stealthily working my way through the long grass and fern towards him. There was still a battle taking place, and the copper was taking out several of my team. 'Shit,' I thought, 'I'm gonna get shot in a minute.'

Then, arriving at my intended position, I took aim at the off-duty member of Hawaii Five-O stood in the deep trench. I came to a kneeling position and then went trigger happy, firing an abundance of paintballs, each one hitting him either in the chest, on his goggles or splatting his helmet.

Two of my station pals, Dan and Max, approached from behind, laughing, having both witnessed the annihilation of the copper. None of us were yet satisfied, so all three of us approached the trench and each shot a further barrage of paintballs from our hoppers onto his chest, legs, helmet, goggles, arms and back.

"Arrrgh, f**k! B*****d! Arrrrrrrgh! Jesus," he shouted as he crouched to the ground, adopting the foetal position to try and protect himself. For a moment, I thought the copper had Tourette's too!

After ceasing fire, I couldn't help but say, "Book him, Danno. No, in fact tag him and bag him!"

Moments later, the nearby marshal, who'd also witnessed our assault on the copper and was chuckling at the harsh number of paintballs we'd fired off, blew his whistle. The copper was the last troop from Team 'B' to be 'K.I.A', and he crawled from the trench, mumbling some colourful language in our direction. Dan, Max and I all laughed out loud.

Max, for some reason, possessed a real dislike of police officers, and said, "Blimey, you'll have so many bruises later today, people will think you've been roughed up by corrupt police. Oh, sorry, you *are* police, aren't you?"

"F**kin' paramedics," he replied under his breath.

"F**kin' police," Max retorted.

Later that day, Conner joined my colleagues and I in a nearby pub for a pint, and while blurting out various verbal tics, explained some of the funny situations he'd gotten into as a result of his Tourette's. He had us howling with laughter, and took no offence whatsoever.

What's This For?

This next incident once again involved Izzie and I; as I told you, we always had a good laugh and plenty of banter together. This story involves the presence of an amazing young man in his late teens, who had Down's Syndrome. He wasn't the patient, he was the son of our patient.

We were dispatched to a lady in her late thirties, complaining of abdominal pain. Upon our arrival and entering through the front door, we were beckoned to the lounge by the patient's son. There, we found the patient lying on the sofa, grimacing and obviously suffering from significant pain.

After Izzie introduced us both, she began questioning the patient, whose name was Susanna. Meanwhile, I began undertaking a full set of vital observations on her. Looking on was her son, Jeremy, who, as previously mentioned, had Down's Syndrome. He was so smiley and friendly, as Down's people generally are from my experience of working in the ambulance service for thirteen years. Jeremy turned out to be a character that I, and I'm sure Izzie, would never forget!

After completing the first full set of observations on Susanna, Izzie continued asking questions and planning the appropriate treatment. With the paramedic bag fully open, Jeremy became rather intrigued at the contents of said parabag. As I stood by the side of Izzie, who was knelt on the floor beside Susanna laid on the sofa, Jeremy began rummaging through the parabag. He pulled a piece of equipment from the elastic loop and asked me, "What's this for?"

Looking at him, I replied, "That, sunshine, is called a laryngoscope. It's used to shift a patient's tongue to the left when they've stopped breathing, so we can put a tube down their throat and assist them to breathe."

He then *threw* it back into the parabag and pulled out a packaged endotracheal tube, and then asked me, "What's this for?" Again, I looked at him and answered,

"That is the tube that we put down a patient's throat when they've stopped breathing." He then *threw* the tube back into the bag and pulled out a packaged bandage.

"What's this for?" he asked me, as I looked down at Izzie bowing her head and chuckling to herself.

"That, Jeremy," I said, giggling, "is a dressing for bandaging patients who have an injury that's bleeding." He *tossed* the dressing back into the bag and then pulled out a packaged syringe.

"What's this for?" As he asked me that question, Izzie glanced over her shoulder and asked if I would prepare a flush and some morphine.

"Of course I will, hun," I replied to her. Then I turned to Jeremy. "I can show you what that's for, pal. Bear with me." I unwrapped the syringe and began to draw up a vial of sodium chloride for Izzie to flush the cannula she was inserting into a vein in Susanna's arm. As I was demonstrating the purpose of a syringe to Jeremy, he looked on intrigued, and displayed a very happy smile.

Handing the now filled syringe to Izzie, she administered the flush into the port of the cannula. Jeremy was fascinated and showed another beaming smile.

As Izzie continued questioning Susanna, Jeremy then pulled the pen-torch from my shirt sleeve pocket. "What's this for?" he asked.

Once again making eye contact with him, I said, "That, buddy, is for shining into patients' eyes so we can see what their pupillary response is... to keep it simple." 'Better not elaborate any further than that,' I thought.

Rummaging through the parabag once again, he pulled out the Sp02 monitor. "What's this for?"

"That is for measuring the percentage of oxygen in a patient's blood."

Jeremy then started man-handling my hand portable radio, so I removed it from the securing-clip and handed it to him. "Don't press any buttons though, Jeremy. Just have a look at it."

While he was having a good look at the radio, Izzie asked me to prepare some analgesic drugs for her to administer to Susanna, to alleviate her abdominal pain. As I was preparing to do so, Jeremy, to my alarm, pressed the little red panic button located on the top of the radio. I instantly knew what he'd done because it makes a distinct beeping sound and goes into record mode, so that ambulance control are able to hear any conversation occurring inside the property. It's a security feature in case there's a genuine risk to staff safety requiring police attendance.

Izzie and I shrieked. "Oh no!" she said, as I quickly snatched the radio back from Jeremy's hand. He started laughing, prompting Izzie and I to chuckle to ourselves. Susanna, on the other hand, apologised and told Jeremy to sit down, stop rummaging, and keep still.

The funny thing about the panic button, which is very rarely used – in fact it's more likely to be pressed in error than pressed due to fear or panic – is that it's *supposed* to be discreetly pressed, so a potential assailant is unaware that verbal evidence is being recorded; they're not meant to know that the police have been called. However, the controller, unaware whether it had been pressed accidentally or not, would routinely buzz the member of staff's radio and, over the airwave, ask, "Is everything all right? Are you at risk? Do you need the police? Over."

Had it been a genuine threat, the assailant would be alerted to the fact that control had been contacted. That could incite an increase in their threatening behaviour, rendering the whole purpose of the panic button feature, to a large extent, futile!

Anyway, an ambulance controller heard us laughing over the airwaves, and so contacted me on my radio. I explained that there was no risk to us and that *I* had pressed the button in error – I kept Jeremy out of it.

Jeremy continued to rummage for a little while longer... fortunately with no harm done. Phew! He then travelled with his mum to A&E in the back of the ambulance.

While I was driving, I could see into the saloon through my rear-view mirror that, despite Jeremy wearing his seatbelt, he was still within arm's reach of a number of drawers, containing a variety of consumables. With Izzie trying to complete the PRF, I could hear her saying,

"Jeremy, be careful with that, love... No, don't press that button on the ECG machine... Leave that alone, Jeremy... Don't press that switch... Put that down, love."

As I drove to A&E, I was chuckling to myself, occasionally hearing Jeremy repeat the same question to Izzie, "What's this for?"

Confusion

Generally speaking, I consider myself a clear verbal communicator. I also, in the opinion of others as well as mine, possess very good listening skills. As a paramedic or ambulance technician, communication and listening skills are of paramount importance. The role of a paramedic involves being a cardiologist, a midwife, resuscitation officer, a dispensing pharmacist, and the all-important counsellor, to name but a few; all of which require good communication and listening skills.

How ambulance personnel communicate with ambulance control, their patients and their patients' friends and relatives, etcetera, can make all the difference between clarity, confusion, and also how a statement is perceived. For instance, my colleague and I were sat on standby one particular afternoon, when ambulance control contacted me via my handheld radio. "Go ahead, over," I said.

"Roger, can you respond RED to Riverside Crematorium. There's a confirmed 'purple' there. Over," the dispatcher said.

A confirmed 'purple' is an ambulance service term used to describe someone who is obviously dead, and has been for some considerable time – i.e. there's no chance of bringing them back to life!

My humorous reply to a deliberately misunderstood message was: "Are we not a little too late to respond to the patient if they're about to be cremated? It's going to need some serious smelling salts and a heating lamp at the very least."

It's an example of how the dispatcher's request could be perceived in several ways. My response was just a little light humour, accepted with a laugh by the dispatcher.

This next incident involves poor communication and understanding, and what was perceived between us, as the questioning ambulance crew, and the patient, her friends and relatives. Allow me to explain.

Ambulance technician, Joanna, and I were dispatched to a nineteen year-old female who was experiencing the signs and symptoms of a panic attack. What made this call both extremely funny and also quite frustrating, was the lack of clear communication skills shown by the patient and her surrounding friends and relatives. More so their choice of words and sentence structure during their explanation of past and present events leading up to the panic attack, and hence the treble-nine call for an ambulance.

Upon our arrival, we entered the property and proceeded to the lounge, where we were welcomed by several people of either sex. The patient was evidently experiencing the symptoms of a panic attack. Joanna immediately began calming the patient and coached her respirations to bring her fast, shallow breathing under control. Meanwhile, I introduced Joanna and I and then began ascertaining some information from the others present.

"Right, what's happening here then?" I asked. Immediately, a young lady spoke up.

"It's Katie. She's been having family feuds lately, and it's causing her anxiety attacks, quite frequently actually," she said. The sound of the patient, breathing rapidly, resonated round the room. Joanna continued to coach Katie, while I continued to ask questions.

"So, what have the feuds been about? What's the main cause of Katie's angst?" I asked with significance.

"Well, her dad died when she was fifteen, but he died owing her dad over two-thousand pounds. Her dad thinks that Katie should pay the two-thousand pounds that her dad owed her dad. There's other problems, too," she stated. Joanna turned to look at me and, as you can imagine, our eyebrows were furrowed as we contemplated what we'd just heard. Joanna continued reassuring Katie and coaching her breathing rate, while I questioned further.

"Hang on, I'm confused. Her dad died owing her dad two-thousand pounds?" I asked quizzically. The young lady looked at me as if there was nothing to be confused about.

"Yeah. *Over* two-thousand pounds, actually!" she exclaimed. I scratched my head in confusion and said,

"She has two dads? One deceased and one alive?"

"Yeah. Her dad's dead but her mum is married to her stepdad."

"Ahhhh, I see. If you'd have said stepdad, I wouldn't have been so confused," I said, but was thinking, 'For f**k's sake!'

As I continued to ask some more pertinent questions, Katie's breathing became progressively more under control through Joanna's efforts, and she would soon be more than capable of conversing with Joanna and I. But before that, a young man spoke up.

"It's not just the money though, boss. It's about certain members of the family not approving of certain relationships. You know what I mean?" he asked.

'No, I don't,' I thought, but instead nodded at him. I was beginning to think this was going to be a long, drawn-out job.

Once we had Katie's breathing back to normal and were happy with her vital observations, we could have considered our job done and it would have been perfectly justifiable for us to leave at that point; we weren't there to play the role of Jeremy Kyle. However, what I didn't want was multiple crews attending to Katie throughout the day, or Katie becoming a frequent caller for the sake of a family feud. I continued questioning.

"So, what other problems are causing feuds then?" I asked.

"Well—" he began to say, but then Katie interrupted.

"My brother and my sister had babies together, and my stepdad favours one over the other. It's causing lots of resentment in them all," she said. Hearing that, Joanna and I glanced at each other, confusion once again clear from our expressions.

"Isn't that only legal in certain parts of the Isle of Wight?" Joanna asked me with a smile of veiled disgust on her face.

"I thought it was illegal world-wide, hun!" I replied. Katie and her surrounding friends and relatives frowned, before Katie piped up and said,

"Hey? What do you mean?"

"Hillbillyitis... incest," I said in a humorous tone of voice and with a grin on my face.

"Incest? No, no! What I mean by my brother and sister had babies together, is that my sister's partner gave birth on the same day that my brother's partner gave birth. Actually, almost the same time of day," she explained.

While it explained the misunderstanding, both my and Joanna's ears still heard something considerably odd in that sentence. Before I could speak, Joanna beat me to it and said,

"Your sister's partner gave birth the same day as your brother's partner did?"

"Yeah," a voice behind me said. "Her sister's a lesbian. Her partner had a sperm donor." By this point I wanted to go out, come back in and start the whole incident from scratch. I rubbed my face with the palms of my hands and replied,

"Ahhhh, turkey baster sort of thing, you mean?"

"For want of a better, more sophisticated explanation, yeah," he replied.

Then others of those stood in the lounge began chattering amongst themselves. It was indistinct chatter, but after thirty seconds or so I clearly heard someone say, "Kate should really move out, now the baby's arrived, but she said she won't. That's causing even more angst. In fact, both Kate and Julie should move out." Upon hearing that comment, I came up with the best idea I'd had during my shift thus far, and said,

"Can one of you get the kettle on, please? I'm parched, and this family feud is causing a lot of confusion." So two of them left the room, leaving just two or three in the lounge, along with Katie, Joanna and I.

I pondered for a moment. "Right, let me get this straight. Katie and her partner have just had a baby, but some of you think she and Julie should move out of their home now that the baby's come along?" I asked.

"No, no. Billy meant that Kate and Julie should move out so Katie and Cath can live as a couple with their new baby," said a young lad who had been mute up until his comment. For a few seconds my head spun, trying to digest the different names.

"So, Katie and Kate are two different girls? I thought some of you call Katie, Kate and Kate, Katie," I said.

"Sorry, pal. We didn't mean to confuse you," Billy said. I, however, thought, 'Really? You didn't mean to confuse me? You've been confusing both me and Joanna since we stepped foot through the front door!' Instead, I replied with,

"No, it's OK, we're getting somewhere now... albeit *slowly*," with the emphasis on slowly.

Our cups of tea soon arrived, fortunately, as both Joanna and I were in need of it. By now Joanna had undertaken some observations on Kate... sorry, Katie, which were all within normal parameters. She then began completing the non-conveyance form, as Katie didn't need to attend the A&E department; we were happy that she'd be fine. As Joanna completed the form, further confusions arose upon me questioning the group.

"So, what'll happen now then? Are you and Cath going to ask Kate and Julie to look for somewhere else?" I asked. Then Billy piped up,

"You should do, and Kat, too!" he exclaimed.

"Kat?" I queried, having not heard that name during the discussion.

"Yeah. Kat is Cath's friend. She lives with us," Katie explained.

'Blimey, you've got a full house haven't you!' I thought to myself, but instead asked, "So, hands up please, if Kate, Kat, Cath or Julie is in this room," thinking it unlikely, as they'd all been talking about them moving out, but just for clarity. Nobody raised their hands. 'Great,' I thought.

In the background I could hear Joanna asking Katie if she lives here, meaning in the house in which we were all present. Katie, however, must have mistaken Joanna's question. "Yeah," she said. So Joanna documented the current address onto her PRF. Then Billy spoke again,

"Come on Katie, when they're done I'll take you home, and we can have a chat with Kat, Julie and Kate about looking for somewhere else to rent. Don't worry about the money situation, it's not even legal to expect you to pay the money to your dad that your dad owed him." 'Oh, don't start again,' I immediately thought, but then Joanna remarked,

"Take her home? You just said you live *here*, Katie. I've written this address on my paperwork now!" Joanna exclaimed, betraying her frustration. Katie glanced at her and said,

"Not here in this house. I mean in this town."

I rubbed the palms of my hands over my face in despair once again, pretended to cry with frustration and said, "Right, come on Joanna, there's bound to be other calls outstanding. Good luck with the baby, Kate—"

"Katie," she said, interrupting to correct me.

"Yeah, yeah, whatever... sorry. Good luck, and I hope you sort everything out. We've got to go now, all the best. See you, everyone," I said as I grabbed our equipment and hurriedly made for the front door, Joanna rapidly following me.

We put the equipment back in the saloon then clambered aboard the cab and began chatting. "I just hope they haven't called the baby Kyle, Karl with a 'K', or even Carl with 'C' if it's a boy," Joanna mused.

"Yeah, or Kath, Kerry or Kelly if it's a girl," I added. We both laughed, as much out of a sense of relief that this bizarre, confusing treble-nine call was complete.

As we attended to others during the rest of the day, we found that we kept calling patients by a name different to the one they'd given us. We seemed to have Kat, Kate, Katie and Cath etched into our minds!

Joanna and I spent the majority of the day intermittently giggling to ourselves, remembering the confusion of that visit. I still keep in contact with Joanna, via phone calls and texts, and we reminisce about that harmless but peculiarly frustrating incident, and many others, too.

GP Admission

Terry and I were on a day shift and heading back to the station when we were passed a GP's urgent admission to take a patient, Marion, directly to A&E. A GP had visited her at home and arranged for an ambulance to convey Marion to hospital; a straightforward 'job' for us.

We arrived at the address, ambled down the pathway and knocked on the front door. A nicely presented gentleman answered.

"Good morning, sir. How are you?" I asked.

"I'm very good, thank you," he replied. Inside the hallway I observed a holdall, which was obviously packed with enough items of clothing for a short stay in hospital. Then Marion emerged, and so I introduced Terry and I.

"Are we all good to go, sir? Are you both coming to the hospital, until settled?" I politely asked.

"Yes, yes, if that's OK? Thank you," the gentleman replied.

All four of us walked to the ambulance and stepped inside. There, they both sat down. "Do you have a GP's letter at all?" I asked.

"Yes, yes, I do." The lovely gentleman handed me the envelope containing the letter, and I handed it to Terry as he was the attending paramedic. He opened it and began carefully reading it, noting Marion's surname, date of birth, current medical complaint/s, and any other ailments and conditions she had at the time, or had had previously. Also what, if any, significant allergies she had, and what medications she was taking, and so on.

After deciphering the GP's hand-written letter, Terry asked the gentleman, "Have you brought all medications with you?"

"Oh, no. They're in the house. I'll go and get them," he replied. As he stepped off the ambulance, I began undertaking a set of basic observations on Marion. As I did so, she said,

"Oh, it's OK. I've recently had these tests done by the GP."

"That's OK, madam," I replied. "We do a set of tests on everybody that travels with us to hospital by ambulance."

Furrowing her eyebrows, she replied, "Oh. That's fine then, young man."

With a basic set of observations completed, the gentleman returned with a bag of medications in his hand. He then took a seat. "Is June on duty today?" he asked Terry.

"Yes, I saw her this morning. Why do you ask?"

"We're both well known to June from the A&E department. Well, all staff in A&E, really."

"Oh, right," Terry replied. Then followed a further short conversation with Marion and her husband, before I positioned myself in the driver's seat ready to mobilise to hospital. Once arrived and parked up under the A&E canopy, we were soon all walking through the A&E entrance, Terry carrying his completed PRF and Marion's holdall.

Entering the ward, I informed Terry that I was nipping to the loo while he handed over to the duty triage nurse... which just happened to be June. Several minutes later, I walked back through to the A&E department and, from a short distance, I could see June laughing her head off, as too were other staff nurses. I grinned as it's always nice to see fellow professionals looking happy.

Arriving back at the ambulance, I immediately noticed Terry sat down, re-writing his patient report form. "What are you doing? You had hold of your PRF when we walked into A and E."

"Yeah, I know," he said, chuckling to himself. "But... you're not gonna believe this."

"What?" I asked, intrigued.

"The gentleman..."

"Yeah."

"The gentleman... was the patient. *His* name is Marion!"

"No! You're joking?!"

"No, I'm not. I'm having to re-write the PRF and explain why I didn't do a basic set of observations on him. It was June who told me. She's in there laughing her bloody head off, she is!"

"I know, I've just seen her. I didn't think it was because of our patient, though," I said with a chuckle. "Hang on, I'm confused. A GP's admission letter always displays the medical symbol for a female or male. What symbol was on the letter?" I asked because there would have been either the circle with arrow pointing to the right, or the circle with a plus sign.

"The circle with arrow to the right," Terry replied.

"That's the medical symbol for a male, you dipstick!"

"Well, I forgot which was which, didn't I! We never use those symbols on *our* paperwork, and I just assumed Marion was a woman's name. I didn't feel the need to ask whether you could remember or not. Besides, the only person I know of with a girl's name is Doctor Hilary from the TV! Who on earth gives their son a girl's name, anyway?!"

To be fair, the medical symbols wasn't something ambulance staff were taught or used. ECPs maybe. We knew what they were but we didn't use them, and very rarely needed to check someone's gender. Of course, I still made the most of Terry's faux pas.

"Marion and Hilary are just two of an abundance of unisex names, you plonker!"

When we arrived back at the station, Terry had the staff in absolute stitches as he recited what had just happened. And for a couple of weeks after the incident, every time Terry walked into A&E with a patient, the staff nurses addressed him as 'Marion'.

Epilogue

Well, there you have it, a second insight into the *Lighter Side* of working on *the Dark Side*. And there are more of my humorous memories I can share with you here, albeit briefly. For example, the very inexperienced ambulance technician who was approached by the station manager while several members of staff were sat in the mess room with him. On his patient report form he had written only the brief words: the patient is 'FUBAR', 'R.I.P.'.

Earlier that same day, he had attended to a severely maimed man who had suffered severe, multiple traumatic injuries after jumping from the roof of a high-rise tower block. He had fallen to his unfortunate and extremely sad and tragic death. Nothing at all funny in that whatsoever, obviously! However, what *most* of his colleagues did find funny was the typical dark sense of humour revealed after the manager entered the mess room and asked him, "What is FUBAR an abbreviation of? I've never heard of it."

"It means the patient was *F**ked Up Beyond All Recognition*," he answered, "and obviously, R.I.P. means *Rest in Peace*."

He received a severe reprimand for his choice of words on what was a legal document that may well have been referred to during a coroner's inquest!

Then there's the time when an ambulance crew were transporting a team of A&E trauma doctors to a serious, multi-vehicle road traffic collision. The paramedic ordered all of them to 'stay put' until *he* declared it safe for them to get out of the ambulance, because there would be other vehicles arriving and leaving the scene, particularly ambulances transporting patients to A&E.

Rolling up on scene, and with the ambulance brought to a standstill, one doctor – ignoring the paramedic's orders – immediately opened the sliding side door. Simultaneously, an almost brand-new fire appliance – later found to have boasted only double figures on the mileage clock – drove slowly past but very close to the ambulance. Consequently, the firefighter who was driving had no way to avoid scratching his offside door along the sliding side door of the stationary ambulance, causing paintwork damage to both the brand-new fire appliance, and the ambulance.

Needless to say, the doctor got a colourfully worded verbal roasting off the paramedic for ignoring his orders.

Then there's the time a crew were passed a RED call while sat having a cuppa in the mess room. They quickly proceeded to their vehicle and positioned themselves in the cab. While applying the seatbelts, the driver discreetly 'let one go', so to speak. Moments later, before they had even begun mobilising, ambulance control stood them down because a nearer crew had become available.

The driver, fully aware that his crewmate was well known for having a very weak stomach when it came to putrid odours, stepped out of the ambulance, engaged the central locking, and leant against the passenger side door so his crewmate couldn't get out. Stuck in the cab, he began to retch while banging his hand against the window. The severe stench of methane, that engulfed the cab of the ambulance, caused him to vomit all over the window and into the foot-well!

And then there's the time I was called to 'The (anonymous) Hotel Health and Leisure Club', to attend to a young lady who had fallen off the treadmill, fracturing her wrist.

On my arrival, the fitness instructor was providing first-aid to her. As I crouched down beside my patient and the instructor, I took a quick glance at his name badge, pinned to his t-shirt just above the hotel name embroidered on the left side of his uniform.

"How long have you had your work t-shirt for, John? It looks brand new," I said.

"It is new. They were only delivered from the manufacturer a few days ago. Why?"

"Were you aware that the embroidery stitched into your t-shirt says Hotel Heath and Leisure Club?" I said, chuckling to myself.

"What?! You're joking!" he said, pulling at his t-shirt to look at the stitching. "Oh, bloody 'ell."

"You're absolutely right, John. It is a bloody 'ell that's missing," I retorted with a smile.

And finally, that prompts me to finish by telling you about the time I wandered into a property several minutes later than my crewmate, Adele. I had been delayed outside, turning the vehicle around because the house was situated in a cul-de-sac. Adele had already begun questioning and assessing the fifty-five year-old patient about his medical concerns, which were depression and anxiety.

When I joined Adele in the lounge, the gentleman was mid-sentence speaking to her, so all I heard him say was,

"...and just want someone to... erm... share my wife with."

Before Adele even had chance to reply to him, I said, "There's certain clubs you and your wife can join for that sort of thing, mate, where consenting adults throw their car keys on the floor in the middle of a member's lounge... so I'm told, that is! Just Google local swingers' clubs."

Laughing out loud, Adele replied, "No, that's not what he meant, Andy! He has a speech impediment and can't pronounce his 'L's. He meant to say he's very lonely... and just wants somebody to share his *life* with."

"Ahhhh, right. Sorry, pal," I replied.

It was only after Adele and I sat back in the cab and she explained what had been said prior to me joining them in the lounge, that I found out he'd actually said, "I'm very wonely and..."

Anyway, I do hope you've enjoyed reading *The Lighter Side, Part 2,* as much as I enjoyed writing it. Hopefully it has given you a few hours of laughter, and maybe provided some escapism from the stress, strain and worry that life often brings.

If the recent pandemic underlined anything useful, it was that it's vitally important that you keep laughing and smiling as often as possible, because it's very beneficial to your body, your mind and your overall health to have a flamin' good belly laugh.

It does your health and wellbeing the world of good if you can adopt a positive outlook on life, and not allow yourself to take too much too seriously, too often, but instead find something to laugh at; whether that be a book, a sitcom, a comedy film, or simply a humorous observation while you're having a relaxing walk outdoors. After all, laughter really is still the best medicine!

The Lighter Side
Part 3

A Former NHS Paramedic's Selection of Humorous A&E
Handovers

Lightning Source UK Ltd.
Milton Keynes UK
UKHW020631300721
388036UK00013B/1183